The Chelsea Football Book No 5

Over: Gary Locke — Chelsea's Player of the Year.

THE CHELSEA FOOTBALL BOOK NO 5

Edited by Albert Sewell

Stanley Paul, London

Stanley Paul & Co Ltd
3 Fitzroy Square, London W1

An Imprint of the Hutchinson Publishing Group

London Melbourne Sydney Auckland
Wellington Johannesburg Cape Town
and agencies throughout the world

First published 1974

Printed and bound in Great Britain
by R J Acford Ltd, Industrial Estate, Chichester, Sussex

ISBN 0 09 120980 3

CONTENTS

GREATNESS BETWEEN THE CHELSEA GOALPOSTS

From their very beginning in 1905, Chelsea were destined to have great goalkeepers. In the physical sense, the greatest without doubt was the first Chelsea captain, Bill Foulke, a man-mountain of flesh, bone and character, who stood 6ft. 2in., weighed in at 22st. 3lb., wore size twelve boots and bell-tent shorts. He could grasp the ball in one hand and punch it beyond the halfway line with one fist. The high shots came easily to him, and to the low ones he dived with amazing speed for a man of his size, often completing the save with a belly-landing on the biggest paunch ever seen in first-class football.

Foulke was the first showman, the first box-office personality, of Chelsea football, and a clown prince figure of the goalmouth long before he arrived at Stamford Bridge. Three times in four seasons between 1899 and 1902 he played for Sheffield United in the F.A. Cup Final, twice collecting a winner's medal, and he was also capped by England while at Bramall Lane.

Chelsea's first manager, John Tait Robertson, said of their first goalkeeper within a few weeks of Foulke appearing on the London scene: 'As a draw alone, he is worth his weight in gold. He is a veritable wonder, and his astonishing ability has aroused a fever of interest in his doings beneath the bar for Chelsea.'

'Little Willie' – as the first Chelsea fans of 70 years ago were quick to name him – born at Wellington, Shropshire, was 29 when he came to The Bridge. He had a sense of humour to match his giant frame, and to emphasise his physique he insisted that Chelsea's smallest player, a 5ft. nothing winger named Martin Moran, walked on the field alongside him. Nor was it just coincidence that Chelsea's two tiniest ball-boys regularly appeared behind the goal that Foulke was defending.

Such things helped to heighten (and broaden) the image, not only in the eyes of the public but in the minds of opponents, too. Twice in one match a Burton Albion player

failed to score against Foulke from the penalty spot, and after the second miss was reprimanded by his captain: 'You shot straight at their 'keeper.' Came the reply: 'I had to – there was no room on either side!'

Stories of Foulke were legend. It was said that once, when Chelsea travelled up-country overnight for a match, the team arrived in the hotel dining-room to find eleven plates had been emptied. The explanation was simple and devastating. 'Fatty' Foulke had mistaken the time of dinner, arrived ahead of the rest...and done justice to a splendid meal!

Foulke spent only one season with Chelsea, making 34 out of a possible 38 Second Division appearances in 1905-6 before removing his massive frame (by then nearly 26st.) to Bradford City, with whom he was to finish his career. Short though his stay was at Stamford Bridge, he played a truly giant part in putting Chelsea on the football map. Yes, to all who saw him beneath the crossbar here and on other grounds, he was an unforgettable figure – a goalkeeper physically unique not only in the service of Chelsea but in the game itself.

The unenviable task of following Foulke as Chelsea's 'custodian' fell to Bob Whiting, who was given the nickname 'Pom-pom' (after the gun) for the tremendous range he achieved with his goal-kicks and clearances which, on occasions, were known to go first bounce over the goal at the opposite end. His 'keeping helped Chelsea win promotion to the First Division as runners-up in only their second season, and the 34 goals conceded was the best defensive record anywhere in 1906-7.

Whiting played 52 League games for the club, being succeeded late in 1907 by Jack Whitley. Having climbed into the First Division, Chelsea appointed David Calderhead from Lincoln City as manager to keep them in the top class, and it was not many weeks before he was followed on the train from Lincoln to London by Whitley – a goalkeeper who brought with him a wealth of experience, starting with Darwen and continuing via Aston Villa, Everton, Stoke, Leeds City and Lincoln to Chelsea.

The first Chelsea team of 1905 parade on either side of Bill Foulke in the North End goal at Stamford Bridge

Mighty Foulke, the 22st. giant who was 'worth his weight in gold' as a box-office attraction in Chelsea's first season. Here he is wearing the "outfield" colours of Sheffield United

Surprisingly for a player who had been such a wanderer, Whitley became one of Chelsea's longest and most faithful servants. He remained at Stamford Bridge for 32 years – the first seven in goal (127 League appearances) and the rest behind the scenes as trainer-in-chief. Whitley, the 'keeper, was renowned as a great puncher of the ball from packed goalmouths and a spectacular diver at the feet of opponents. In one sense he gave up the boots for the sponge a year too soon; otherwise, he could have collected a 1915 F.A. Cup medal against Sheffield United at Old Trafford.

By then the established Chelsea goalkeeper was Jim Molyneux, who had been signed from Stockport County in the summer of 1910. For the modest fee they paid for him, Chelsea received marvellous value, for Molyneux was their first 'keeper to make 200 League appearances. His grand total of 210 games from 1910 to 1921 would have been considerably larger but for the four-season stoppage of League football caused by World War I.

In the early 1920s Chelsea's last line was occupied by one of the most exciting and least orthodox goalkeepers of the period – the celebrated amateur Benjamin Howard Baker. This famous Corinthian played, on average, nearly one game in every two for the Blues from 1921-26, totalling 92 League appearances for the club. He was a big, bouncing figure who frequently dashed beyond his penalty-area to clear; an all-round sportsman who played good-class cricket and tennis and was English high-jump champion of his time at a record 6ft. 5in.

Howard Baker was a regular Amateur International goalkeeper and twice won full caps for England. He is also on record as the only 'keeper in Chelsea history to leave his line and go to the other extreme of the field to score a goal. This drama occurred two minutes from the end of a First Division home match against Bradford City on November 19, 1921.

Chelsea were awarded a penalty for 'hands'. Jack Harrow, the captain, had missed twice from the spot already that season and did not relish a third, and the shooting of Chelsea's forwards had been so poor all afternoon that none of them fancied their chance either. But one player was bursting to take that kick – and, in a moment of inspiration, Harrow found him and called him up from the far end of the pitch. Howard Baker ran eagerly upfield and, to the delight of what remained of a 25,000 crowd, smashed the penalty past Jock Ewart, Bradford City's Scottish International, to win the match by that one and only goal. But Howard Baker did not keep the job of Chelsea penalty-taker for long; the risks

Jack Whitley, the wanderer who stayed 32 years with Chelsea
Jim Molyneux — 210 League games in Chelsea's goal from 1910-21
Benjamin Howard Baker, Chelsea keeper who scored with a penalty

were demonstrated a few weeks later, when he tried again from the spot against Arsenal at Highbury — and saw his shot saved.

Besides playing for Corinthians and Northern Nomads, Howard Baker kept goal for four big League clubs, Preston North End, Liverpool, Everton and Chelsea. The two-way

Howard Baker is seen, bottom right, with a group of other Chelsea stars at the 1967 FA Cup Final banquet. Standing, left to right: Andy Wilson, George Mills and Billy Russell. Front left, Nils Middleboe. Front centre, Bob Thomson

affection between him and Chelsea was to be long-lasting. He became a successful businessman in Cheshire...and when Chelsea reached the 1967 F.A. Cup Final one of their many former players who attended the after-match banquet was Howard Baker.

For consistency over a long period, Sam Millington merited a place high in the list of notable Chelsea goalkeepers. Coming into the side in 1926-27, he played 223 out of a possible 294 League games over the next six years, his season-by-season appearances numbering 32, 40, 38, 38 again (in promotion year from Division II, 1929-30), 40 and 35.

But even Millington's fine record was exceeded by Chelsea's next goalkeeper, Vic Woodley. Born in Wiltshire and an amateur on Reading's books, he left Windsor & Eton to turn professional for Chelsea at the age of nineteen in the summer of 1931 for what was then a £10 signing fee.

Towards the end of season 1931-32, Woodley replaced Millington in seven matches. With rare exception, he was to be first-choice 'keeper through the thirties up to the outbreak

Sam Millington — Chelsea's regular goalkeeper from 1926-32

of World War II in September 1939, by which time he had become the first Chelsea goalkeeper to reach the milestone of 250 League appearances (actual total 252).

Stamford Bridge in the thirties provided the unusual situation of a club possessing two International goalkeepers – to be repeated in modern times by Peter Bonetti and John Phillips. For in the summer of 1933 Chelsea bought Johnny Jackson from Partick Thistle after a dazzling display by him on his Scotland debut in a team that had beaten England 2-1 at Hampden Park on April 1.

Indeed, on the strength of that performance Jackson (who liked to be known as Jake rather than Johnny) began the 1933-34 season by displacing Woodley, who had been Chelsea's ever-present goalkeeper the previous winter. But in only his sixth game for his new club Jackson suffered a serious head injury when making a typically dare-devil dive at the feet of a Huddersfield forward and had to go to hospital, so Woodley took over again.

In the three seasons up to the outbreak of war Woodley played for England 19 times, an appearance rate never previously reached by a goalkeeper in International football. Class was stamped all over his game, and the presence of Jackson in the Chelsea Reserves served to keep him forever on his toes. For here were two tip-top men duplicating the goalkeeper position for Chelsea at one and the same time – friends and rivals each so good as to play for his country. And although Jackson was mostly a club reserve, that did not prevent the Scotland selectors keeping faith in him, and he gained two more caps as a Chelsea player.

Jackson's best Chelsea season was 1934-35, when he made 27 of his 49 First Division appearances for the club. But in the shadow of Woodley, he was mostly the happy-go-lucky stand-by – and rated the best golfer among goalkeepers and, without doubt, the best goalkeeper among golfers. Jackson always said the finest save of his career was not on the football field but when he jumped into the sea at Douglas, Isle of Man, to help a girl swimmer who was in difficulties. In due course he married the girl he had rescued.

Vic Woodley, who won 19 England caps in three seasons before the war

Scotland's Johnny Jackson was Chelsea's other international keeper in the Thirties

Signed from West Ham in 1946, Harry Medhurst is still going strong in the service of Chelsea, now as physiotherapist

Woodley played at Wembley for Chelsea as well as for England – in the 1944 League South Cup Final which was lost to Charlton by 3-1. His last match for the Pensioners, as Chelsea were then known, was against Tottenham in December 1945. Woodley was then transferred to Derby County, and within four months went to Wembley again, collecting an F.A. Cup winner's medal with them against Charlton. Later he joined Bath City as player-manager and, on retirement, became a publican in the West Country.

Chelsea's goalkeeper when League football was resumed after the 1939-45 war was W.H. (Bill) Robertson, but in December 1946 manager Billy Birrell set up an exchange deal with West Ham that was to have long-lasting benefit to the club both on and off the field. In that transaction, centre-forward Joe Payne moved from Stamford Bridge to Upton Park and goalkeeper Harry Medhurst travelled in the reverse direction. Apart from a six-months' break at Brighton, where he ended his playing career, Harry has been with Chelsea 28 years – the first five seasons between the posts (143 First Division appearances), then returning from Brighton as assistant-trainer and subsequently serving as head trainer and now physiotherapist.

At 5ft. 9in. and 10st. 10lb. Harry belonged in the 'small but good' category of goalkeepers. In physical contrast, his successor was a young giant of 6ft. and 12st. 10lb – the second Bill Robertson in five seasons to wear the green jersey for Chelsea's first team. 'Big Bill' was a player who very nearly failed to 'arrive' in senior football, because after being signed from Scottish junior club Arthurlie in July 1946 he spent five years in the second and third teams at Stamford Bridge and had despaired of ever breaking through when Billy Birrell named him for a surprise League baptism at home to Liverpool in April 1951.

No debut was ever made in more testing circumstances. With four matches to play, Chelsea were rooted at the foot of the First Division table, six points behind the third-from-bottom club with only one game in hand. To have even the thinnest chance of staying up, they needed to win those four games...and with the club's destiny largely in his hands, Robertson fainted in the dressing-room only half an hour before kick-off against Liverpool. But with the aid of a stiff whisky and strong smelling-salts, trainer Norman Smith got him on his feet in time to play. Liverpool were beaten 1-0 and Robertson kept his place as well as a clean sheet. Those other three matches were also won and, by nothing less than a football miracle, Chelsea escaped relegation by .044 of a goal.

For the next six seasons Robertson remained almost permanent first choice, but no-one seeing his state of nervous anxiety on the day of his debut would have dared to believe he would play 199 First Division games for Chelsea and win a League Championship medal in season 1954-55, when he shared the goalkeeping duties with a fellow-Scot, Charlie (Chick) Thomson.

In November 1956 Chelsea paid a new record fee for a goalkeeper when Ted Drake went to Coventry City and signed England's Reg Matthews for £20,000. So yet another name was added to the list of Internationals who have guarded the Chelsea goal, and once out on the field Matthews was among the most agile and lithe 'keepers in the business.

Bill Robertson — a dramatic debut, then 199 First Division games in Chelsea's goal

Reg Matthews cost Chelsea a new record goalkeeper fee of £20,000 when signed from Coventry in 1956

But often in the hour or so before kick-off Reg was gripped by nervous tension; a pile of half-smoked cigarette stubs on the dressing-room floor beneath the peg where Matthews hung his clothes was evidence of that.

Over five seasons from 1956-1961 Matthews made 135 First Division appearances for Chelsea, and in October 1961 he moved to Derby County in a £10,000 transfer.

Midway through Matthews' reign as Chelsea's No.1, manager Ted Drake one day opened a letter postmarked "Worthing." It was from a mother recommending that her 15-year-old son, who had played for Worthing and Brighton Schools, 'might make you a useful goalkeeper,' and asking whether he might be given a trial.

That letter and the trial that followed brought to Chelsea the finest of all in their long line of top-class goalkeepers — Peter Bonetti. From his League debut in a 3-0 home win against Manchester City on April 2, 1960, 'The Cat' was to be automatic choice for thirteen seasons. In November 1973 he became the first player in the club's history to complete 600 senior games, and consistently brilliant form allied to that record number of appearances worthily earned him the fans' vote as 'Chelsea's greatest-ever player.'

Who will ever forget Bonetti's supreme goalkeeping which denied Leeds victory in the 1970 F.A. Cup Final at Wembley, then his courage in carrying on virtually on one leg, after injury in the replay at Old Trafford? Without that most heroic of all Bonetti's displays, Chelsea would surely never have returned next day from Manchester with the Cup in their possession for the first time. And without that stepping stone back into Europe, they could not have gone on to another cup conquest a year later, when Peter Bonetti, again in masterly form against those European maestros, Real Madrid, made an outstanding contribution to Chelsea's first European triumph in the Cup-Winners' Cup Final in Athens.

Seven England caps; honours in the League Cup (1965), F.A. Cup (1970) and Cup-Winners' Cup (1971); Chelsea's first 'player of the year' in 1967; the record number of first-team appearances (604); those were the bare statistics of Peter Bonetti's wonderful career at the end of season 1973-74. By then John Phillips had emerged as his likely long-term successor and as next in line to add to the fascinating story of Chelsea goalkeepers down the years.

'The Cat' pounces again...and it's another spectacular save by Peter Bonetti, only player in Chelsea history to make 600 first-team appearances

RTSHOES
WH

CFC

...AND NOW, JOHN PHILLIPS

'For the first time I am playing for Chelsea on merit. Previously, I was in only when Peter Bonetti was injured, and the difference is enormous.' That was John Phillips talking late last season (1973-74), when it appeared that the record-breaking reign of 'The Cat' as Chelsea's first-team goalkeeper was at last over, leaving Phillips in the role of permanent successor...and glad, after all, that he had soldiered on through three frustrating years of mostly reserve-team football.

John Phillips, now 23 and just on 6ft tall, was born at Shrewsbury into a footballing family. Both his father, Roy, and his grandfather, Tom, were professionals with Shrewsbury, at centre-forward and full-back respectively. But John himself was an early disappointment. 'Until I was eight I used to run away from the ball. I hated the game. When I did start to play I was interested only in scoring goals. But one day, just to be doing something different, I decided to go in goal. I was ten then and I've been a 'keeper ever since.

'My father and grandfather spent hours making me practise the many aspects of goalkeeping. They encouraged me enormously, teaching me the basics of the job, and without them I would never have been where I am today.'

Although no written contract was signed, John agreed verbally to join Shrewsbury Town on leaving school. 'Stoke City showed interest but I had to turn them down. As it happened, I would have been waiting behind Gordon Banks. Instead I eventually found myself understudying Peter Bonetti here at Stamford Bridge.'

Phillips signed for Shrewsbury manager Arthur Rowley at fifteen and became an apprentice. The club's next manager was Harry Gregg, of Manchester United and Northern Ireland, one of the game's finest goalkeepers. Says John: 'He was an adviser and a friend, but he encouraged me to play in my own style. I still keep in touch with him and he remains my severest critic. I remember him once telling me to keep press cuttings but to look at them only when I was depressed.

My mother keeps the cuttings and I've never forgotten that advice.'

Two years later, Shrewsbury's first-team goalkeeper was sold. John, at 17, was promoted to his position. He still remembers his home debut, the third game he had played for the club. Indeed, it would be hard to forget. 'Early on, I was bouncing the ball, waiting for the defence to move out. The opposing centre-forward played the ball as it hit the ground, won the chase for possession and scored.'

Although John Phillips did not know it at the time, it was his determination after that particular mistake that convinced Harry Gregg he was a real prospect. 'I knew then that he had the right temperament,' said Gregg. With Shrewsbury the young goalkeeper also showed bravery to the point of the suicidal. He recalls another incident, although, not surprisingly, it is a hazy recollection: 'An opponent dribbled to the by-line, pulled the ball back and I dived for it. So did their centre-forward, and our heads met. Everyone was so persistent in asking me if I was alright that it began to annoy me. Then in the second half I put the ball down for a goal-kick, took three paces backwards and fell flat on my back. The next thing I remember was waking up in hospital, and there in the next bed with a broken nose was their centre-forward.'

While at Shrewsbury, Phillips was called up for trials with England Youth at Lilleshall. He appeared in practice games against West Bromwich Albion, Burnley and Coventry. Finally, he was told that he was in the squad to tour the Netherlands, but postal confirmation was never received. Fortune had smiled again. If the letter had arrived, he would not have been eligible to play for Wales in years to come through parental qualification.

In October 1969, after 51 appearances for Shrewsbury, John was signed by Tommy Docherty for Aston Villa for £30,000. 'He was a tremendous inspiration to young players. He took me aside early on and said simply, "I don't like cowards or cheats. As long as you are neither, we'll get along fine." But Villa were a young side then. Players were just beginning to emerge like Bruce Rioch, transferred last season to Derby County for £200,000.'

John Phillips makes a brave save at Stoke

Phillips keeps out this effort by Martin Chivers on his full International debut for Wales at Wembley in May 1973. But he couldn't prevent a 3-0 England victory

Suddenly, it all turned sour at Villa Park. Tommy Docherty was sacked. John Phillips played in the following game and was subsequently dropped. Aston Villa were then relegated. 'I would have found myself back in the Third Division as a reserve goalkeeper. But during pre-season training in August 1970 I was called in and told to travel to Chelsea.'

Tommy Hughes, the Chelsea reserve goalkeeper, had broken his leg on tour in Holland, and John was wanted as cover for Peter Bonetti. The transfer fee was £25,000 and Phillips was delighted with the move. 'My goal, if you'll excuse the pun, had always been to play for a First Division side and here was a chance at least.'

Two months later, in October 1970, his big opportunity arrived. Bonetti was injured and Phillips was picked to play against Blackpool at Bloomfield Road. It was to be a debut hard to forget. 'At the end of the first half we went back to the dressing-room three goals down. It seemed to be one of those days, and I could imagine Chelsea fans back home thinking that we had lost because of the reserve goalkeeper. But what a transformation in the second half. Twenty minutes from the end we went mad. We couldn't stop scoring. We won 4-3 and the 'Chelsea flop' became the 'Chelsea revival.' It was the first of 18 first-team games I played that season. They included the quarter-final and semi-final of the European Cup-Winners' Cup.

'I hoped and prayed that I would play in the Final against Real Madrid in Athens. But Peter Bonetti had recovered from pneumonia and Dave Sexton chose the experienced player. I felt sick. It was the biggest disappointment of my career.' Phillips, impatient in his quest for regular football, asked for a transfer — a request that was turned down.

'I wasn't unhappy with Chelsea. I was unhappy at being a reserve. By 1972-73 I was in a similar situation with Wales — capped for the Under-23's against England and Scotland, and second in line behind Gary Sprake for full international honours. But at the end of the season the breakthrough came and I played against England at Wembley in the Home Championship.'

The Phillips close-up — Dave Sexton takes a cine-camera to record a first-class save by John at Chelsea's training ground at Mitcham

This penalty save, from Gerry Francis in the FA Cup at home to Q.P.R. last January was 'the greatest moment in my career so far,' says John

This was not the first time John had appeared at Wembley. 'In 1966 I was a ball-boy in the semi-final of the World Cup, England against Portugal. That was the first time I had seen the famous stadium. I found it smaller than I had expected but the turf was like a lawn, like a carpet.

'I had no nerves, playing against England. Admittedly, I was excited. All I wanted to do was get out there and play. The atmosphere gave me a special lift, and once the game started there wasn't time for anything but concentration.

'I don't usually have nerves but I do have superstitions. I avoid stepping on the white lines around the goalmouth. I keep my gloves on if there is no score against us at half-time. I come out of the tunnel anywhere but second and I always put my shorts on last.

'It wasn't until the beginning of this year that I really sensed I had a chance of keeping a regular place with Chelsea. Three first-team players were dropped, including Peter Bonetti, on New Year's Day away to Sheffield United. We knew we had to win, and we did, 2-1, but for the first time I felt nervous. I knew that I couldn't afford to make any mistakes.

'The next game was against Queen's Park Rangers in the third round of the F.A. Cup at Stamford Bridge. It brought the greatest moment of my career so far – that penalty save from Gerry Francis. Somehow I felt that things were going my way, and guessed the right way to dive.

'But I think an even better save last season was against Newcastle up at St. James' Park. It is one of my favourite grounds along with Maine Road, White Hart Lane and, naturally, Villa Park. It was a wet day, with pools of water lying everywhere. The ball came across about eight yards out. Malcolm Macdonald's left foot met it on the half-volley and the rumours about his 'left peg' are not idle. I managed to reach the shot with my right hand and push it over the bar. That save satisfied me more than any other I have made.

'I have never had a goal-keeping idol, and like to think I have my own style. I respect Pat Jennings, of Spurs, for his remarkable consistency. That is the most important aspect about a goalkeeper. He can perform brilliantly for 89½ minutes and then make an error. It is the slip that will be remembered. The rest will be forgotten.

Phillips at full stretch to prevent 'Supermac' – Newcastle's Malcolm Macdonald – reaching a high cross at Stamford Bridge last March

ZEPHYR

'I rate Peter Shilton, of Leicester City, and Jennings as Britain's top two. Nevertheless, I feel the standard of goalkeeping in this country is not as high as many people think. Although I never saw them, football fans still talk about the likes of Frank Swift and Bert Trautmann. Since Gordon Banks gave up the game, there don't seem to be many real 'greats' nowadays.

'People often ask me how I became known as 'Sticks' at Chelsea. It originated from a comment by John Hollins. I always wear gloves and he used to ask me if I had my 'sticks' on. The insinuation was that the ball stuck to the gloves like fly-paper. I certainly don't object to that.

'Now, for the first time, I feel settled at Chelsea. One cannot foresee the future, but I've been lucky. I haven't been seriously injured and I've had some breaks. But even though it may have seemed that I was becoming established as Chelsea's No. 1 'keeper in 1973-74, I felt the situation was not finally settled because Peter Bonetti is such a great competitor...and only by consistently good performances could I hope to hold onto my place. My hope is that the fans at Chelsea will respect me for my own ability. If I can be as good as Peter and stay at Chelsea for as long as he has, then I shall be a happy man. And that is what matters.'

The gloved hands of 'Sticks' Phillips signal that all is well as this shot by Peter Lorimer passes wide in last season's 1-1 draw at Leeds

SUNNY DAYS & STARRY NIGHTS WITH CHELSEA

Geoffrey Green (The Times)

A selection of 'special occasion' Chelsea match reports by the Association football correspondent of The Times, by whose courtesy they are reproduced.

Date:	Saturday, 18 May, 1963
Match:	League Division 2
Result:	Sunderland 0, Chelsea 1

BIZARRE VICTORY TRUE TO CHARACTER

How perverse is football and how tantalizingly unpredictable are Chelsea! Seldom do they follow the book or the obvious lines. They lose when they ought to win; they win when they should lose. They invite at once affection in the neutral and sleepless nights for their exasperated followers.

Quite in character, then, was this vital win at Roker Park in the gusty, squally north-east on Saturday. The result is that the situation is left on a knife-edge, for one of these two sides must accompany Stoke City into the First Division next season. Yet there is nothing more that Sunderland can do about it. The future is out of their hands.

Their programme complete, they now face 48 hours of anxious waiting, hanging on the outcome of Chelsea's match against Portsmouth at Stamford Bridge tomorrow night. If Chelsea conquer them, promotion is theirs after only a single season out of the top drawer, leaving poor Sunderland beaten on the very post by decimal goal average for the second successive year. However, anything less than victory will do Chelsea no good. The future is in their own hands, for Sunderland can only stand and gape helplessly and hopefully. That is the situation in a large nut shell.

As it was, Sunderland missed the chance on Saturday of deciding their own fate. All they needed was a draw. That would have sent them skipping joyfully back to the First Division — where, as a club and by tradition, and with over a million spectators at Roker this season, they truly belong. Yet they missed the boat when everything was loaded in their

favour. Now they may pay the price for a tense and often frenzied effort to settle the affair.

Everyone realised that taut, dangerous situation on Saturday. You could sense it in the 48,000 crowd – smaller than expected because of fear of crushing and physical discomfort; you could see it in the players themselves, in their drawn faces and jerky anxious movements.

As if to brush away all these fears, the wind this day blew a half gale out of its north-east lungs. But this last act of the elements proved to be a mistaken kindness. Rather than clearing the air, it made the battle more difficult, more untidy and more the child of passing incident.

It was, indeed, a raw, ragged, rugged struggle. There was little football; brawn dominated brain; tempers were frayed and the referee almost blew the pea out of his whistle while he kept jotting names in his notebook with all the regularity of some train spotter.

Yet the battle did disclose the character, fibre and integrity of this young Chelsea side, especially in defence. Everything was against them – the dedicated crowd; the bleak record of not a single point gained away from Stamford Bridge since Boxing Day; and throughout a tempestuous second half, the bulging wind itself and the sun. And, to make matters even more demanding, they were reduced virtually to 10 men when Upton hobbled to the wing with a severely twisted knee some 20 minutes from the end.

Out of all this emerged a brave, bizarre, and unexpected victory by a single goal, scored midway through the first half. Even this precious touch had a scrappy, frayed look. It was almost Chelsea's first serious attack, begun and carried on by the tenacious, combative McCreadie, their left-back.

From this sudden advance little Harmer forced a corner on the right. Tambling produced a dipping in-swinger, the ball was deflected by Ashurst, and the next second it was in the roof of the Sunderland net, prodded home by the alert Harmer somewhere off his waistline. It was scarcely textbook. But what could Chelsea care at such a time? It was decisive. It was the end.

Tommy Harmer scored only one first-team goal for Chelsea, but what a gem it was! This is it, as tiny Tom prods home a corner-kick in the last game but one of season 1962-63. Without it Chelsea would not have won promotion the year after being relegated

Promotion night – May 21, 1963. Skipper Bobby Tambling shoots Chelsea's second goal and the first of his own foursome in the 7-0 victory over Portsmouth

The rest was frenetic and fragmentary. Sunderland struggled with their bodies rather than their minds. Even artists like Anderson and Herd were now submerged in the rush. The sharp edges of Crossan were blunted by Venables; the wingers, Davison and Mulhall were handcuffed, and Sunderland stunned themselves into defeat.

The heroes, in fact, were Chelsea. McCreadie and Shellito – an England back of the near future – each was Horatio. So, too, was Mortimore, more ruggedly. Tambling was the man for the quick break and almost stole two more goals near the end to make nonsense of all Sunderland's patternless hammering. At the very last breath, too, the acrobatic, unbeatable Bonetti made a remarkable diving save that erased some of his tragic errors under the Chelsea crossbar this season.

But on a day when the ball blew about crazily like cricket bails in a storm, only one man looked the part of an artist in attack. He was Harmer, the minute imp, so small and frail he was almost unnoticed. He, at least, found time to stand on the ball, attempt some pattern, and try to smooth out the wrinkles. It was that sort of a match, when points and not poetry counted.

SUNDERLAND – Montgomery; Nelson, Ashurst, Anderson, Hurley, McNab, Davison, Herd, Sharkey, Crossan, Mulhall.

CHELSEA – Bonetti; Shellito, McCreadie, Venables, Mortimore, Harris, Blunstone, Kevan, Upton, Harmer, Tambling.

REFEREE – L.J. Tirebuck (Halifax)

Date: Tuesday, 21 May, 1963
Match: League Division 2
Result: Chelsea 7, Portsmouth 0

CHELSEA SWEEP BACK TO FIRST DIVISION: HARMER THE GUIDING HAND, TAMBLING THE STRIKER.

After one season of exile, Chelsea last night returned to the First Division when they swamped Portsmouth in the final match of the season. They never seem to do things by halves.

All they needed was a victory, and a 55,000 crowd arrived at Stamford Bridge expecting a night of twanging nerves and perhaps even defeat. Yet a goal in 90 seconds by Kevan — perhaps one of the most important he has scored and his first for Chelsea — relieved all the tension.

From that moment Chelsea unwound in a trice, could see the horizon of victory, and swept through the night adding goal after goal. When the score was six, with still 25 minutes to go, the chant of the crowd was 'We want seven.' And finally they got it when Tambling, living one of his great matches, crashed a rocket into the roof of the Portsmouth net for his own fourth goal.

So poor Sunderland, for the second year running, are left behind in the Second Division, now beaten on goal average. But there was no question about last night. With still four minutes left the pitch was invaded by practically every small boy in West London, probably mistaking the referee's whistle for a free-kick as full-time. For a brief moment there were visions of the match being abandoned through lack of discipline and Chelsea having to relive another night.

But sanity prevailed, the roar of the rest of the crowd of 'Off, off, off' finally won through, and it was moments later when the young men could at last give vent to their feelings. The field became a human mass as the Chelsea players fought for their dressing-room. But Tambling, the captain and the hero, was caught by the tide and tossed shoulder-high like a blue cork in a turbulent sea.

It had been no match on a worn, brown field with an elusive ball. Yet one man mastered it, little Harmer, of the matchstick legs and the cool footballer's brain. He was the man who smoothed out any remaining fears that may have lurked after Kevan's early strike.

By the quarter-hour Tambling cracked in number two from Blunstone's flick. At the half-hour, in Greaves fashion, he went like a lizard through the grass, beating three men swiftly to plant his left-foot shot beyond Armstrong. There it was at half-time with Chelsea clearly already well on course.

Within half an hour of the second half four more goals had come. Superb pace, which left the defence standing, and a left-foot shot gave Tambling his third goal. Then a passage of interplay between Tambling and Blunstone gave Blunstone an opening. Next a penalty by Venables, after Brown had desperately pulled down Tambling, and finally that last thunderbolt from Tambling.

So we look back and see how Chelsea, once seven points ahead of this Division, kept their Cosmopolitan clans in suspense to the last. Now they can look forward, but, if Kevan and Upton were used at the last as ramrods through the centre, they are not really what Chelsea will need in the First Division.

Harmer, of course, remains the wise elder statesman, but his future in the top class is problematical. He is the sort of man, though, that Chelsea need in the years ahead, years that should see the emergence of Tambling, Shellito and Venables as real figures. As for Portsmouth, this night they were merely the other team.

CHELSEA – Bonetti; Shellito, McCreadie, Venables, Mortimore, Harris, Blunstone, Kevan, Upton, Harmer, Tambling.

PORTSMOUTH – Armstrong; Gunter, Wilson, Brown, Dickinson, Campbell, Barton, Gordon, Saunders, McCann, Lill.

REFEREE – R. Aldous (Ipswich).

So Chelsea return first time to the First Division. Manager Tommy Docherty doesn't need a microphone to tell the fans: 'We're back to stay!'

Date: Saturday, 11 April, 1970
Match: F.A. Cup Final
Result: Chelsea 2, Leeds United 2

CHELSEA RESTRAIN LEEDS' CONTROL

This had to happen one day. At last, after extra time and two hours of punishing excitement on a sand heap, Wembley threw up an unfinished F.A. Cup final and for the first time since the stadium became the Old Vic of English football in 1923 – its stage now torn, tattered and down-at-heel like some Thespian fallen on bad times – the gleaming trophy itself was left unclaimed in the Royal Box.

As the thread of a memorable match unwound, this perhaps was as well. After so much that was heroic it would have been sad to be left with a loser, for as the Chairman of the Football Association said later: 'This was not a classic. It was an epic.'

Now these two fine sides must look unflinching into each other's eyes again. The place will be Old Trafford Manchester, the date April 29, the time 7.30p.m. Which brings us to a curiosity. The last final ever played outside London was in fact at this same Old Trafford. The date was April 24, 1915 and the losers were Chelsea in their first appearance at the climax of this competition.

Perhaps the fates this time have something different up their sleeves to make amends. But Leeds truthfully should have won on Saturday but may yet pay for missing the bus, or, should we say, being robbed by Chelsea's lucky star which was in the ascendant.

Twice the Yorkshiremen were in the lead, only to be caught unexpectedly on each occasion – four minutes from the interval and finally again four minutes from the end of normal time, only moments after they themselves had gone ahead to 2-1.

The Cup then looked bound for Leeds at last as Jones put a cross shot past Bonetti's dive after a rebound to Clarke's header to the foot of the post. Bremner at that second did a joyful double somersault; there were dancing white shirts everywhere on the field, and the steeped West banks of the stadium holding the massed Leeds clans exploded. Even Don Revie, their manager, had to be restrained by two burly policemen as he tried to join his happy players on the touchline.

Yet within moments there was Hutchinson to plant a flying header past Sprake's right hand as Hollins chipped a free-kick from the left to the near post. It was a well-rehearsed tactic that now caught Leeds flatfooted at the last breath, their concentration perhaps already deflected by the thoughts of approaching celebration. Yet if Leeds commanded much of the play Chelsea, fired by Cooke's clever dribbling as the match wore on, showed an undying spirit that kept them alive. Few sides comes from behind twice against Leeds.

That is the way these things sometimes go, and having hammered the Chelsea goalposts three times in the afternoon through Gray and Clarke, Bremner and his men must still be wondering how much more they have to do to win at least one prize from a momentous season. It may yet come in a strange way, for they now go to face Celtic in the second leg of the European Cup semi-final at Hampden Park on Wednesday with a single goal to recover. But they now face a foe maybe psychologically unhinged by their sensational 3-1 defeat at the hands of Aberdeen in Saturday's Scottish Cup Final.

That, of course, is hypothetical. What must be beyond dispute is that here, technically — remembering the killing conditions — was the finest Cup Final seen at Wembley since the war, better even than Manchester United and Blackpool of 1948 and lacking only the emotional impact of the last 20 minutes of the Stanley Matthews fiesta of 1953.

Now the 100,000 crowd had everything from A to Z. For our money we also had two soft goals before the interval, reminding us again that Wembley still remains both a graveyard of goal-keepers and a stage of fear where the tiniest mistake may prove disastrous.

Drama was in the wind from the start. The first open hint came after 20 minutes when Charlton got above Bonetti and the rooftops to head Gray's corner. Harris and McCreadie stood guard on the Chelsea line and McCreadie should have cleared easily. But the ball, instead of bouncing, squatted like a wet sponge to slip under his foot and creep home almost apologetically.

With Giles and Bremner, the generals, commanding the central areas with wide, sweeping passes and Gray running poor Webb dizzy all through with mazy footwork so that the full-back must have felt he possessed webbed feet — Gray was later quoted Man of the Match — Leeds should have then nailed their enemy.

But as half-time approached it was their turn to blunder. As Houseman hit Hutchinson's side-header first time from the edge of the box, Sprake looked to have the low ball covered. But again the pitch proved to be the villain of the piece. The shot skidded, then slowed up to creep through and under the goal-keeper's dive inside the posts. It was tragic as Sprake hung his head in disbelief.

Yet soon enough he made amends at the change of ends with two point blank saves from Hutchinson which led to Hunter also blocking a final strike somehow or other from Osgood, on the Leeds line. Still, it was Yorkshire who continued to carry the fight, mounting a steady bombardment which saw Bonetti emerge only fractionally behind Gray in overall merit as one of the heroes of the battle.

It all belongs to the past now, but some of Bonetti's saves were magnificent. Add to that the shots from Gray and Clarke that almost splintered the Chelsea crossbar, and a remarkable last ditch block by Webb, in extra time as Giles volleyed at an open goal, and the debt Chelsea owe to their rearguard can scarcely be measured. For Webb that moment alone repaid all his other torment.

Extra time itself was an added cruelty. Players dropped like flies with cramp as there followed other breathtaking saves and escapes at each end. It was almost unbearable.

CHELSEA – Bonetti; Webb, McCreadie, Hollins, Dempsey, Harris (Hinton), Baldwin, Houseman, Osgood, Hutchinson, Cooke.

LEEDS UNITED – Sprake; Madeley, Cooper, Bremner, Charlton, Hunter, Lorimer, Clarke, Jones, Giles, Gray.

REFEREE – E. Jennings (Stourbridge).

Wembley, April 1970 – Dave Sexton leads the Blues out of the tunnel, in step with Don Revie, his Leeds counterpart, But it was to be another 18 days before Chelsea won the FA Cup in the longest of all Finals

Date:	Wednesday, 29 April, 1970
Match:	F.A. Cup Final Replay
Result:	Chelsea 2, Leeds United 1

CHELSEA SEIZE CUP IN EPIC FINAL

The treadmill is over. A new name is on the F.A. Cup and it belongs to Chelsea. One of the most punishing finals in modern history – perhaps all history – begun at Wembley with extra time over a fortnight ago, ended at Old Trafford, Manchester, last night, again in extra time.

Looking back over the long struggle, we can now say that Chelsea came three times from behind to match the League champions of last year and finally snatched the winner 14 minutes in the extra period. Any side that can do that against such a worthy foe from Yorkshire deserve their trophy.

So, with an historic touch about it, Chelsea have at last won the prize which they first played for at Old Trafford in the final of 1915, when Sheffield United beat them. And when Lord Derby that day handed the cup to the Yorkshiremen of Sheffield, he said: 'You have played with one another and against one another for this cup. Play together for England now!'

Those words may now be echoed in a different way, for there were six men on the pitch last night who will leave on Monday with England's World Cup party for Mexico. They, too, must play for England.

This was no match for weaklings. As the sun dipped out of sight over Old Trafford's mighty stands, it seemed to take with it flaming streamers of the day; and it left behind a bonfire. Here was a match of gleaming steel, mostly with the broadsword, which was used with impunity by both sides and allowed to be used by a referee who would have a short life in Latin America.

From the earliest stages bush fires of anger flickered across the field – briefly, it is true, before they died. Yet all the time there was a cauldron simmering just beneath the surface as the match steadily increased in excitement and vigour, with Chelsea fighting back in the second half out of a dark hole. By half-time, indeed, Leeds looked to have the match wrapped up and neatly labelled for themselves.

After the 2-2 draw at Wembley, Chelsea fell behind for the third time in the 1970 Final when they met Leeds again at Old Trafford. Then Peter Osgood headed this magnificent equaliser from Charlie Cooke's chip...and once more it's extra time

David Webb jumps for joy after heading the Cup-winner at Old Trafford

CFC

PRIVATE
21
NEWS
TON

In a surge of attacking football between the twentieth minute and the half-hour they had Chelsea by the throat. A terrific tackle by Dempsey stopped Clarke bursting through on a long pass from Lorimer; Lorimer flashed a right-foot thunderbolt inches wide; Jones flicked the side netting close in after a move down the left between Giles and Gray. And all this was heavily underlined when McCreadie cleared off the line from Lorimer, with Bonetti stranded.

This could scarcely last – the more so when Bonetti was felled heavily as Jones crashed into him on a long cross from Madeley. After lengthy repairs to the Chelsea goalkeeper, who later emerged again as one of the heroes of the night, it was seen that Bonetti was limping on one leg. His left knee was heavily bandaged after the interval.

But by then Leeds had at last taken the lead they so well deserved. It came nine minutes from the change of ends. And what a great goal it was. It began with Clarke, who ghosted his way past three tackles across midfield, slipped a through pass to Jones, who, going like a steam engine, held off the close attentions of Dempsey, eluded the converging tackles of Hollins and McCreadie and fairly thundered a right-foot shot to the top of Bonetti's right-hand corner.

It was a goal from the past, as old-fashioned as the horse and carriage. It revived memories of Ted Drake in his heyday. But slowly Chelsea, who had been caught time after time in the close meshes of their over-complicated game, began to open out and find themselves. Up till then their football had been soft at the edges and blank as unwritten paper on a pitch bulldozed for speed.

There was some vicious tackling. Boadicea might have been on parade with the knives on her chariot wheels. There were moments when the football was as raw as uncooked meat. It was like a hoarse declaration of protest as the 62,000 crowd showed their anger at the other man's guilt. At last, with half an hour left, Chelsea began to find their tidemark.

With 25 minutes left Hutchinson was booked. But by now Osgood, Cooke and Hollins had begun to play beautifully, moving the ball smoothly in flowing moves of unexpected angle. Suddenly, they began to burn some magic fuels. Here

Ron Harris, First chelsea captain ever to receive the FA Cup, is chaired by triumphant team-mates, left to right: Peter Osgood, John Hollings, Ian Hutchinson, Peter Houseman, Marvin Hinton and David Webb

Jubilation Day for Chelsea and their followers as the team arrive back in Fulham Road next day with the FA Cup

was the echo of Wembley again. Having been largely over played there for a long period as now, they began to come at the right moment. The change in the tide, and the feeling it communicated to the packed company, gave out an intense radiation. It almost dislocated the senses.

Where once the great steam roller of Leeds had driven forward, with Giles and Bremner putting Jones, Gray and Lorimer into full stride, and with Clarke adding some highly cultured and sensitive touches, it had all been one way. Now it was the elegant Osgood, the elusive Cooke and the non-stop Hollins who oiled Chelsea's wheels at last.

With 10 minutes left they suddenly were level. Theirs, too, was a beautiful goal; more complicated, more finely ingrained, more liquid and created virtually out of nothing. Here was the poetry of football and it came with a magical exchange of passes between Hollins, Hutchinson, Osgood and then the hard-running Cooke. Over came Cooke's perfect chip and there was Osgood infiltrating from the left to the blind side to head a magnificent goal.

So it was extra time, as at Wembley, and with only seconds to go to the last change-round before yet another replay, there came one of Hutchinson's long throw-ins from the left. Up went Jackie Charlton and, poor fellow, his backheader swung across a crowded goalmouth. There was a sudden surge of figures and, ironically, it was Webb, the man who had been tormented at Wembley, who was first up to head the winner.

That was it, and though Hinton came on as a substitute for Osgood in the last five minutes as a tactical stroke for Chelsea, and though Bremner moved up front, and though brave Leeds threw in all their last resources, it was no good. Having looked the winners, they were now the losers. Leeds, like Sisyphus, have pushed three boulders almost to the top of three mountains and are now left to see them all back in the dark of the valley.

CHELSEA – Bonetti; Harris, McCreadie, Hollins, Dempsey, Webb, Baldwin, Cooke, Osgood (Hinton), Hutchinson, Houseman.

LEEDS UNITED – Harvey; Madeley, Cooper, Bremner, Charlton, Hunter, Lorimer, Clarke, Jones, Giles, Gray.

REFEREE – E.T. Jennings (Stourbridge).

Date: Wednesday, 19 May, 1971
Match: European Cup-Winners' Cup Final
Result: Chelsea 1, Real Madrid 1

REAL SHOW ALL THEIR OLD ARTISTRY TO DASH CHELSEA'S HOPES

After two hours of pulsating and racking struggle, the eleventh Cup-Winners' Cup final still stands undecided. In the Karaiskaki Stadium last night Chelsea and Real Madrid found themselves involved in a dramatic climax which saw the Spaniards snatch victory away from the Englishmen during injury time to save themselves at the very last breath.

So they replay once more in this same beautiful setting tomorrow night; and if ever a reprieve was deserved it was deserved now. Real, in a tremendous grandstand finish, were thoroughly worthy of another shot for the cup. Chelsea no doubt will be feeling sore and robbed at this moment. Yet it was nothing like moonlight robbery.

Real were the footballers. They showed this not only for long periods in the first half, but over their fighting finish and all through extra time, when their artistry made them the masters. The Spaniards have established a technical and psychological advantage which they could well turn their way in 48 hours' time. Meanwhile much will depend on injuries after a hard battle. These will not show themselves until the morrow.

The way Real came back from what appeared to be the darkest of shadows was admirable. After showing all their old graces in the opening half, they suddenly found themselves behind 10 minutes after the interval. A sudden move between the lively Cooke and Boyle saw Boyle's low cross picked up by Osgood, in spite of a nudge in a crowded defensive area, to shoot the loose ball home hard and low, left-footed to the corner.

For the next 20 minutes or so Chelsea at last seemed to begin to believe in themselves. Until then there had been some delightful four, five and six-man moves — back heels, flicks and delicate touches — which reminded one of the Real Madrid of other days. At moments they seemed to be taunting Chelsea like a matador teasing the bull.

But once Osgood — in perhaps the only good thing he did throughout the night — had put Chelsea ahead, then at last Cooke took up the running. With swaying footwork and fine control, he inspired some of his colleagues finally to show what they had in them.

All the time the Chelsea defence had done their job bravely in the face of much of the Spanish subtle criss-cross passing and sensitive approach play. Amongst them Webb was a hero; so too was Boyle, and in the final stages of extra time Bonetti, with two or three reflex saves.

But if Cooke did so much to try to inspire a Chelsea win, in the end it was perhaps Webb, more than anybody who kept them in with a chance in the replay. In the closing moments of extra time he made at least two magnificent tackles to save Chelsea's bacon as the last minutes of the night unwound.

It was in this splendid stadium, a stone's throw from the sea, with all the flags flying under a dark blue night sky, that a full house of 41,000 people swayed with the battle.

This indeed was a Greek amphi-theatre for a play which has not yet ended. Certainly, it would have been a Greek tragedy if Real had lost, for in men like Amancio, Pirri, Velasquez and Zoco, they had the outstanding artists. It was Zoco, pushed up into attack in the last quarter of an hour of normal time, who in the end rescued Real.

With the Chelsea defence and the whole crowd looking at their watches, a last desperate attack was launched by Amancio and Pirri. Up went the ball, Dempsey miskicked and there was Zoco in like a flash to shoot past Bonetti. There was not time to restart. Now they must go through it all again.

CHELSEA – Bonetti; Boyle, Dempsey, Webb, Harris, Hollins (Mulligan), Hudson, Cooke, Weller, Osgood (Baldwin), Houseman.

REAL MADRID – Borja; Luis, Benito, Zoco, Zunzunegui, Pirri, Grosso, Velasquez, Perez (Fleitas), Amancio, Gento (Grande).

REFEREE – R. Scheurer (Switzerland).

Date:	Friday, 21 May, 1971
Match:	Athens – European Cup-Winners' Cup Final, Replay
Result:	Chelsea 2, Real Madrid 1

NOW CHELSEA ADD TO PRIZE LIST

Chelsea, winners of the F.A. Cup a year ago, are the new holders of the European Cup-Winners' Cup in succession to Manchester City and have now become the fourth English club to lift this prize.

After a swaying, dramatic first act of two hours a couple of days ago, the odyssey was at last ended in the Karaiskaki Stadium here tonight. Real Madrid, after a brave finish over the last half hour, are left behind to pick up the pieces of a forthright challenge that began last September. Two goals, in seven minutes by Dempsey, and then Osgood, just after the first half hour, laid the foundations of a victory that Chelsea had to fight hard to hold over the final stages.

With this victory London has taken its fourth trophy in a season – after the Championship title and the F.A. Cup with Arsenal, the Football League Cup with Tottenham comes this latest achievement for Stamford Bridge.

There were changes from the first match in the character of much of the play and tactics. Chelsea decided on a 4-2-4 pattern of play with Baldwin brought in as a second striker to help Osgood in the middle. In the first half this made a sharp difference, upsetting the Spaniards and helping Chelsea to achieve a mastery. As for Madrid, they had Pirri on parade again surprisingly, his left wrist heavily bandaged, but they dropped the veteran Gento and Perez, who were on the wings last time.

This gave us something new to chew on. The goals were splendidly taken. After Borja had punched out a corner-kick from Houseman while under heavy pressure from the aggressive Webb in the 31st minute, Dempsey volleyed home a great right-foot shot to the roof of the net from fully 15 yards. The centre-half could scarcely have scored a more important goal in his career.

Seven minutes later Chelsea struck again. Baldwin took a pass from Harris, his captain, slipped a through ball to Osgood, who dummied and shot low past Borja's left side to the corner of the net from the edge of the penalty-area. Chelsea looked home and dry.

The first half had shown them in new colours. No longer were they ravished by the elaborate style and subtle

ASSOCIATION
CUPWINNERS
1970
FOOTBALL LEAGUE

inventions of the Spaniards as they had been at times 48 hours earlier. Real's white feathers in that opening half were ruffled and almost plucked from their backs.

Chelsea were practical and functional and there was a brighter radiance about their whole game as they went harder and faster for the ball. Men like Hudson, who had shown little in the first game, came more into their own. Both sides will look back on their battle over three hours and a half spread across two nights. At times both were good and both were bad; there is no absolute about these things. In the end it was a survival of the fittest, with Chelsea proving themselves on that score.

Yet it took one magnificent save by Bonetti with only four minutes left as he made a flying dive to catch a diving header from Zoco – the man who had saved Real on Wednesday; and then a superb tackle by the irrepressible Webb, who kept out Amancio almost on the goal line with Bonetti left on the floor.

Chelsea's hero again was Cooke, always hungry, always running eagerly, full of zestful control as he became the midfield commander-in-chief, driving his men on and matching it all with a boldness of thought in his distribution. Webb, too was powerful again in defence, but Osgood, playing only his fifth match in four months, understandably faded over the last stages, to be substituted by Smethurst.

Once Fleitas, in a brilliant individual piece of work, dribbling in after gathering a rebound from Webb, had shot Real within range with a quarter of an hour to go, we reached the climax of skill, inspiration and excitement.

CHELSEA – Bonetti; Boyle, Dempsey, Webb, Harris, Cooke, Hudson, Weller, Baldwin, Osgood (Smethurst) Houseman.
REAL MADRID – Borja; Luis, Benito, Zoco, Zunzunegui, Pirri, Grosso, Velasquez (Gento), Fleitas, Amancio, Bueno (Grande).

REFEREE – A. Bucheli (Switzerland).

Triumph in Athens, May 1971. Ossie has scored the goal that beats Real Madrid in the Cup-Winners' Cup Final

Another open-top bus drive through West London's crowded streets as Chelsea bring home their first European prize

FAMOUS CHELSEA 'FIRST' AND RULE CHANGES

Chelsea were the first club in football history to score a victory without kicking a ball. They arrived in the Football League – voted in at the annual general meeting in London on May 29, 1905 – with a team which had been assembled from scratch in barely a month, and not until the beginning of the next season did that Chelsea side make their first appearance in the public eye.

The acceptance of a club before they had so much as sent a team on the field remains a unique form of entry to the Football League, and in a variety of ways Chelsea have contributed more 'first occasions' than most to the story of British football. In addition they have influenced a surprising number of changes in the administration of the game.

To begin with, in their opening season of 1905-6, something happened to Chelsea which caused an important amendment to the F.A. Cup rules. All other Second Division clubs had been excused from the competition's qualifying rounds, but as the season's Cup schedule had been planned before it was known whether the new London club would be playing in the Football League or the Southern League, Chelsea were called upon to qualify.

The first two hurdles were cleared, but in the third qualifying round – at Crystal Palace, venue of the Cup Final itself in those times – Chelsea were knocked out by Palace by seven goals to one, which is still the club's heaviest Cup defeat. By way of explanation, there were special circumstances...very special. On the day of that Cup-tie, Chelsea were required to play their best available side in a League match, and while 'Chelsea proper' were taking two points off Burnley by the only goal at Stamford Bridge, a second eleven was scraped together for Cup duty at Crystal Palace. The sequel was that the Football Association passed a rule insisting on full-strength teams being fielded in all rounds of the Cup.

In the spring of 1910, Chelsea did things in the transfer market which were also to have lasting repercussions. Facing relegation to the Second Division, they made desperate efforts to save themselves in the last two weeks of the season, signing nearly half a team of new players, among them such stars as Bob Whittingham, who brought terrific shooting power with him from Bradford City, English McConnell and Marshall McEwan.

What Chelsea could not buy, however, was time, and despite the new acquisitions they went down. That was not the end of the matter. Although no rules had been broken by the eleventh-hour transfer plunge, the authorities did not like the precedent, so a regulation was passed preventing players transferred after March 16 (recently amended to the second Thursday in March) taking part in matches affecting championships, promotion and relegation. The rule they introduced read: 'After March 16 in each season transfers shall not be sanctioned if the committee consider such are sought for the purpose of obtaining an unfair advantage.'

Chelsea took only two years to win back their First Division place but, finishing nineteenth of twenty, they were again due for relegation at the end of the 1914-15 season. But the next time they went into full-scale League action — in 1919, after World War I had caused a four-year break — they were still in the top division. Once again Chelsea were involved in a unique situation.

In 1915 Manchester United finished one point and one place above them, but there was an enquiry into a match between United and Liverpool which proved the result had been arranged to beat bookmakers operating fixed odds. Seven players, four of Liverpool, three of Manchester United, were found guilty and suspended, and because the 'fixed' result had affected final placings, Chelsea were reinstated in the First Division in 1919 on its extension from 20 to 22 clubs.

In season 1926-27 a sixth round F.A. Cup replay at Ninian Park after Cardiff City had drawn 0-0 at Stamford Bridge, produced an incident — at Chelsea's expense — resulting in the penalty-kick law being altered. Two goals down, Chelsea were awarded a penalty, and as Andy Wilson placed the ball on the spot he was astonished to see the Cardiff goalkeeper, Tom Farquharson, standing in the back of the net, with arms outstretched and his fingers entwined in the mesh. As Wilson shot, Farquharson leapt forward into the field of play and saved. Chelsea lost the tie 3-2 (ironically by a penalty at the other end), and after Cardiff had gone on to Wembley and taken the 'English' Cup out of the country for the first and only time, the game's legislators altered the laws to compel goalkeepers to stand still, on the goal-line, until the ball is actually kicked from the spot.

THE YEAR CHELSEA WON THE LOT!

There has never been a collection of "football firsts" quite like Chelsea won in 1954-55 to celebrate their fiftieth anniversary. They were Football League champions for the first time, and three other league titles came to Stamford Bridge. The Reserves won the Football Combination, the "A" team were champions of the Metropolitan League and the Juniors won the South-east Counties League. This was the official club photograph — directors, players and staff, 61 in total — to commemorate Chelsea's most triumphant season, trophies and all.

BACK ROW: Boyd Nisbet, Ron Tindall, Bob Edwards, Derek Gibbs, Paul Berry, John Sillett, Roy Cunningham, Bobby Laverick.

THIRD ROW: Dick Foss (Youth Manager), Dick Spence (Assistant Trainer), Dick Whittaker, Peter Tuck, Alan Hetherington, Alan Rule, Stan Wicks, Roy Merrifield, Tony Nicholas, Les Allen, Wally Bellett, Len Casey, Harry Medhurst (Assistant Trainer), Fred Hanney (Hon. Physiotherapist).

SECOND ROW: Jack Oxberry (Trainer), Stewart Davidson (Assistant Manager), Bobby Smith, Alan Dicks, Syd Tickridge, Peter Sillett, Owen Medlock, Charlie Thomson, Bill Robertson, Brian Pickett, Stan Willemse, Derek Saunders, Ron Greenwood, Peter Brabrook, George Mills ("A" team Manager), Albert Tennant (Coach).

FRONT ROW: Ted Drake (Manager), Eric Parsons, Seamus O'Connell, Jim Lewis, Mr. Joe Bennett (Director), Johnny McNichol, Mr. Charles Pratt (Vice-Chairman), Roy Bentley (Captain), Mr. Joe Mears (Chairman), John Harris (Vice-Captain), Mr. Leslie Mears (Director), Ken Armstrong, Mr. Len Withey (Director), Frank Blunstone, Les Stubbs, Ray Kitchener, John Battersby (Secretary).

SEATED ON GROUND: Colin Court, Roy Fergey, Jimmy Smith, Andy Bowman, Cliff Huxford, John Compton.

In 1928-29 Chelsea were among the clubs foremost in the experimental numbering of footballers. Their players wore them for the opening home game against Swansea Town (and won 4-0, the season's biggest score at Stamford Bridge), although it was 1939 before the League introduced compulsory numbering.

Coming to more modern times, Chelsea were the first club to take advantage of the ending of the ban on air travel in connection with League matches. Manager Ted Drake decided that after a Good Friday match at Newcastle (won 2-1) on April 19, 1957, the quickest way home would be the best in preparation for the next day's game against Everton. That high-flying journey back to London was followed by high scoring – Everton were beaten 5-1, and on Easter Monday Newcastle crashed 6-2 at Stamford Bridge, giving Chelsea a total of 13 goals and a maximum six points over the holiday.

Chelsea were largely responsible for the League and the F.A. introducing the regulation which calls for the declaration of teams at least half-an-hour before kick-off. It followed an incident on the way to their first F.A. Cup Final appearance at Wembley in 1967. In the fourth round, Chelsea drew 1-1 in a tense, all-ticket tie away to Third Division Brighton. The sending-off of John Boyle meant that for two thirds of the match ten men faced eleven, and there was some 'feeling' between rival Scottish managers Tommy Docherty and Archie Macaulay.

When the teams met again at Stamford Bridge four nights later, both managers played a tactical cat-and-mouse game in the dressing-rooms beforehand. Neither wanted to be the first to reveal his line-up, and the players were actually on the field before the team changes could be announced.

Authority took the view that such manoeuvres were not in the best interests of the game, which is why League regulations now stipulate: 'Clubs must hand copies of a list of names of players taking part in the game (including the name of the nominated substitute) to the referee and a representative of their opponents in the presence of the referee in his dressing-room at least thirty minutes before the advertised time of kick-off.'

Chelsea pioneered the soccer magazine-type programme at Christmas 1948; they were contestants in the first European match transmitted back to England and shown live on closed-circuit television (their Fairs Cup semi-final play-off away to Barcelona in May 1966 which was relayed via six large screens to nearly 10,000 spectators at Stamford

Bridge); and in October 1972 Chelsea showed how to counter the problem of pitch invasion by spectators. They became Britain's first club to erect wire fences behind the goals — a most effective deterrent which others, faced by this growing hazard, have been surprisingly slow and reluctant to adopt. And at Stoke last January, Chelsea took part in the first First Division fixture ever staged on Sunday.

Doubtless there will be other Chelsea 'firsts' to come — further rule-changes in which they will be instrumental to the overall benefit of the game. Indeed, they might have inspired another major alteration to the transfer regulations at this year's annual meetings of the Football League and Football Association, for Chelsea believe the time has come to revise the rule which Cup-ties a player to one club each season.

Through lack of support from other clubs, Chelsea's futuristic thinking on the subject never reached the proposal stage on the 1974 agendas, but that should not prevent them continuing to campaign for such an amendment. After all, as transfer fees continue to rise, it becomes increasingly logical that star players should be permitted to appear for more than one club per season in Cup matches, just as they are in League football. Provided, of course, as Chelsea's suggestion insists, that there are safeguards to prevent teams being strengthened in this way for semi-finals and finals.

IAN BRITTON– TOMORROW'S BILLY BREMNER?

Chelsea, it seemed, posed one imponderable situation after another through season 1973-4. One question to which the answer will never be known was: Might the domestic upheaval that followed have been avoided if 5ft. 5in., 9st. 2lb. Ian Britton had played against Leeds United on December 15? When Leeds came to Stamford Bridge that day, Chelsea could well fancy their prospects of becoming the team to end the visitors' unbeaten run of 19 matches since the start of the season.

With the dismal opening spell at last behind them, Chelsea were now coming together again as a side. Themselves undefeated for six games (four wins, two draws), they had climbed to halfway in the table, with Britton starring in midfield in the last four of them — home wins against Everton, Southampton and Leicester City, in which a total of ten goals were scored, and an away draw with Arsenal.

But each match poses different problems. Every week, every manager in the game gambles to a degree on his team selection, and that day against Leeds Dave Sexton decided to bring back Peter Houseman, while Britton sat out the ninety minutes on the substitute's bench. In the event, if first-half chances had been taken it could have been Chelsea's day, but Leeds won 2-1. That was to be the first of four consecutive defeats, and a result that, in retrospect, turned the course of Chelsea's season.

Britton was recalled immediately after the Leeds match and established a regular place. Even in the club's struggling second half of the season, here was a young player who grew in stature week by week. Probably his finest display of all was on Queen's Park Rangers' quagmire in the F.A. Cup third round replay. Despite ankle-deep mud, Britton never stopped running, chasing, challenging, and in the depths of disappointment at such early Cup defeat, his was a performance to lift Chelsea hearts.

Ian Britton arrived on the first-team scene as substitute against Derby County at Stamford Bridge on December 30,

1972, replacing the injured Ian Hutchinson at half-time. He came up through the reserves on this recommendation from assistant-coach Dario Gradi: 'He is a real little 90-minute buzzer. Ian covers every inch of the ground, wins the ball and knows how to use it. He has been our most consistent player all season in the Combination side — a mighty midget if ever I saw one.'

As Stamford Bridge fans observed at once, the description fitted the 18-year-old Scot who, on his first appearance, had the considerable satisfaction of a part in Chelsea's equalising goal by Peter Osgood. Through the following March and April he was a member of the first team and, with rare exception, played regularly last winter from November march. Long before the end of that 1973-74 season the tick could be placed against his name as yet another successful product of Chelsea's junior section.

At which point it is appropriate to bring in Youth manager Ken Shellito on the subject of Ian Britton. He says: 'As long as a player is good enough, you don't have to consider whether he is 5ft 6in. or 6ft 5in. In Ian's case possibly we made his size something of a problem at first, but by the time he settled into the first team last season we were no longer aware of the fact that he was usually the smallest player on the field. We were too busy watching what he was doing with the ball, and off it.

'Ever since he came to us as a boy his approach has been the same — he's enthusiastic to learn all the time, a hard worker and a lad who gets enormous enjoyment out of playing the game. I think he conveys this to the crowd, too. He has a big appetite for training and coaching, as well as for playing, and really came on last season. At a time when things were not going well for the side generally, it was quite an achievement for a lad of nineteen to play so many consecutive matches.

'Ian came down from Scotland as a winger, and began in that position in our youth side. Then, one day, we had a trial at Mitcham and were short in midfield. He filled the gap and at once looked a natural for the job. He has played midfield ever since.'

Britton has not consciously modelled himself on any particular player. 'I have always played my own style, but when I first came into Chelsea's senior side my football was inhibited by nerves and by a lack of self-confidence. I like to

Little legs, maybe....but a big jump

be involved all the time, but at first playing alongside stars – especially Peter Osgood, who was always something special to me – I tended to give the ball too early.

'I only had to hear a player call for a pass and I would give it without thinking whether that was the best ball for the situation. But as my confidence grew match by match, I found myself playing as I want to play, holding the ball when I feel it should be held, passing when I think a pass is on, and generally doing what I feel to be right.'

For Ian, who was 20 last May, playing first-team football with a major club is a boyhood dream come true. As a schoolboy right-winger back home in Dundee his ambition was always a career in football, and early in 1969 Chelsea scout John King watched him playing for a Scottish Sunday League side called Hillside Rangers.

'Luckily for me, it was one of my best matches,' recalls Ian, 'and I was invited down for a trial that Easter, just before my 15th birthday. I was too young to sign then for Chelsea, but returned the following Christmas and became a junior here. A season and a half later, in July 1971, I signed professional.'

As a boy in Scotland, Britton admired two English teams in particular, Chelsea and Manchester United. His heroes in those sides were Osgood and Denis Law. Now a player himself, one of his most memorable games, he says, was for Chelsea against Manchester United in the final home match the season before last. Another of his schoolboy idols made his farewell appearance in first-class football that day. 'I shall always be proud to say I played once on the same field as Bobby Charlton,' says Ian.

Another match he has good reason to remember was against Southampton at Stamford Bridge last November. He scored his first Chelsea goal and 'at 5ft. 5in. I felt 10ft. 10in. when that one went in.'

Modestly he puts his immediate ambition as 'earning a place in the Chelsea side,' but before last season was half-way through, it was not difficult to see Scotland Under-23 honours coming his way. His hard running, enthusiasm and total commitment already mark him out as a potential successor to Billy Bremner in Scotland's midfield. In style, skill and size there is a similarity that was up for comparison when Chelsea drew 1 - 1 at Leeds last February.

Ian takes on Martin Buchan, of Manchester United, in a Scot versus Scot tussle for possession

Scars of battle. Britton needs stitches at the end of a match

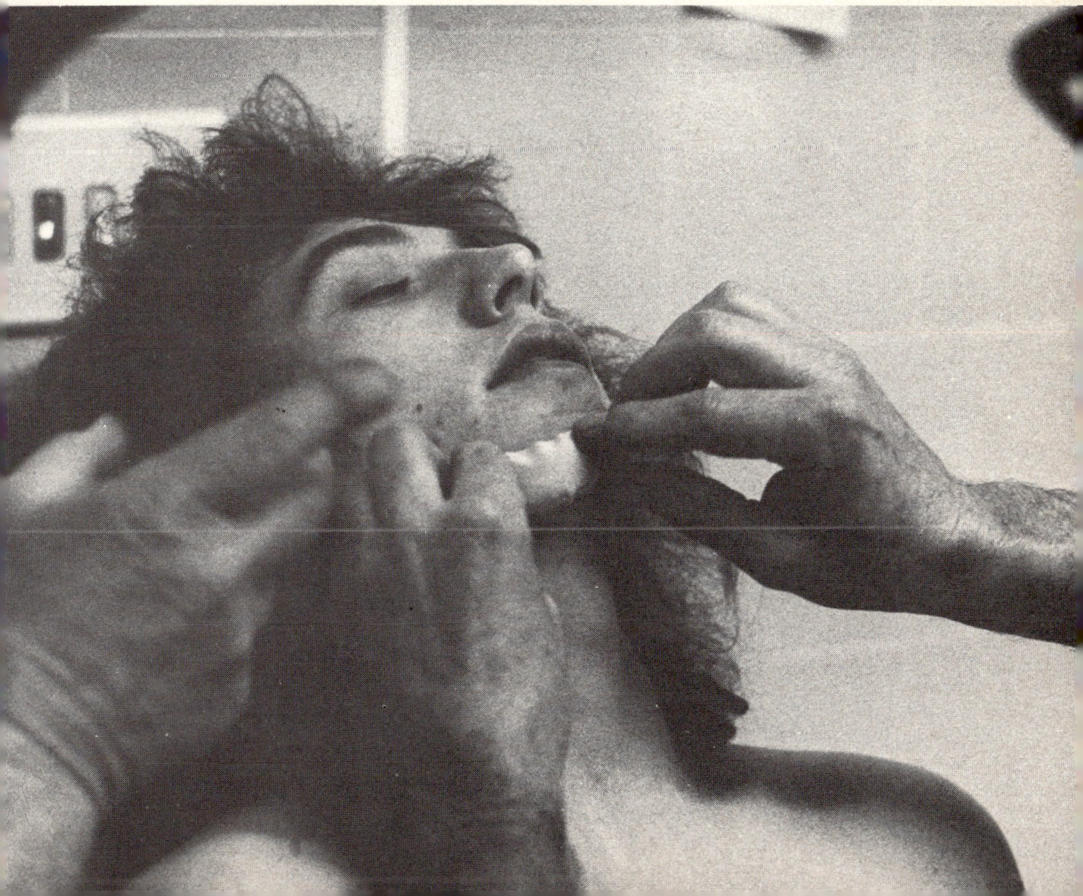

The star and fellow-Scot Ian Britton resembles in size and style — Billy Bremner in 1970 FA Cup Final action for Leeds against Chelsea at Wembley

Since he came to Chelsea, Britton has had the benefit of one of the best coaching combinations in the game, and how well he has responded is reflected in the progress he has made. Ken Shellito was the first major influence while Ian was in the juniors; in the reserves he advanced in the hands of Dario Gradi; and when Britton took the next step up the ladder into the first-team squad he came under Dave Sexton's tuition, quickly learning to curb a natural desire to chase every loose ball and to concentrate on those he could catch.

One of his most treasured possessions was won on tour with the Chelsea Youth team in Belgium at Easter 1972. 'Eight or nine teams took part in the tournament, and when it was over the organisers gave me the 'best player' award. Winning that medal out of nearly a hundred players was very pleasing,' says Ian.

He shares 'digs' with Gary Locke near Chelsea's training ground at Mitcham, and has stayed there ever since he came down from Scotland. Away from football, golf is his other sporting interest, with the occasional round after training with fellow-Scot Steve ('Jock') Finnieston.

Ian also plays golf back home in Scotland in the summer. As a Chelsea junior, he returned to Dundee every six weeks but now, with the added responsibilities and stricter schedules that come with life as a professional, homegoing is limited to the close-season or the occasional week-end after a trip North to Newcastle.

Ian was not the first member of the Britton family to seek a career in English football. Elder brother Billy, now 25, also came down for a junior trial with Chelsea, but for him it did not work out, so he went back over the Border and signed for Forfar Athletic, later moving to Brechin.

Scottish talent has been recognised in Chelsea football ever since the club was founded in 1905, and Ian Britton helps to maintain that tradition. In the re-shaped team of 1974 and beyond, there is unlimited scope for a young player of his ability and potential. For the moment, let Dave Sexton have the last word about him: 'Ian is a player who really earns his place. He is as enthusiastic to learn as he is to play; he fits the description of the 'typical Scottish ball-player' and by nature is the sort of boy you love to have with you.

'At first he lacked confidence, and because of that I didn't think he would get in as many senior games as he has done so soon. But he overcame the problem to a large extent last season, and when he becomes fully aware of what he can do, he has it in him to become a great little player. No...let me change that and say a 'great player,' because nobody here is conscious of his size any more. Tomorrow's Billy Bremner, did you say? Yes, I think that suits Ian Britton rather well.'

THE SEASON THAT LASTED FOR YEARS

In times of success, the months, the matches and the moments to savour pass all too quickly. For instance how swift and fleeting were Chelsea's Cup triumphs at home and abroad in 1970 and 1971, how distant those heady days now seem.

In reverse, when things are not going well, time drags — and for Chelsea 1973-74 was a season which, in the mind at least, lasted for years. In the simplest terms, it began badly and got worse, with items on the credit side of the ledger heavily outnumbered in the opposite column. Long-term, probably the brightest aspect was the way Gary Locke enhanced the previous year's promise at right-back, joined on the left late in the season by 16-year-old John Sparrow, who showed enormous potential for his age. On the evidence of what we saw, it was not stretching the imagination too far to feel that here, in embryo, was a partnership, home-grown and nurtured in the club's prolific youth section, that could take care of the full-back situation at Stamford Bridge for ten seasons or more.

John Phillips, latest in a long line of pretenders, emerged as the man ultimately to succeed Peter Bonetti between the Chelsea goalposts. Micky Droy, bringing height and weight at centre-back, gained valuable first-team experience, but the season ended with Chelsea still lacking real midfield command and up front, although they were paradoxically among the highest First Division scorers, there was urgent need for class and crowd-pulling charisma after the transfer of Peter Osgood.

Within the club and on the stands and terraces, there would be few who did not lament what developed as "the Osgood affair," for players of his calibre are all too rare to part with lightly. Chelsea were always more reluctant to transfer Osgood than Alan Hudson, who seldom seemed in the mood last season to play up to his known capabilities — or, at least, not until he was wearing the red and white stripes of Stoke City.

They weren't all here at the finish, but this was Chelsea's first-team squad at the start of season 1973-74. Back row, left to right: David Webb, John Dempsey, Bill Garner, Ian Hutchinson, Micky Droy, Peter Osgood, Alan Hudson. Middle row: Marvin Hinton, Ron Harris, Gary Locke, Eddie McCreadie, Tommy Baldwin, Steve Kember, Chris Garland. Front row: John Phillips, Peter Houseman, Ian Britton, John Hollins, John Boyle, Peter Bonetti

Another major off field problem in 1973-74 was that one season without a main stand East-side became two. Events proved that, in modern industrial Britain, the estimate of August 1973 as the original opening date was vastly optimistic, and instead of housing nearly 12,000 spectators, it remained all season a £2,000,000 skeleton of steel and concrete.

By losing at Derby and Burnley, both games by the only goal, and then 2-1 at home to Sheffield United, Chelsea made their worst of all post-war starts. After those three matches, they were the only First Division club without a point, but the anxiety was eased by three victories in the next four games, including a double against Birmingham.

Between these results was a 0-1 defeat away to the Champions Liverpool, a match in which Bonetti gave one of the finest displays of his career, topped by a marvellous penalty save from Keegan. The "Cat" needed to be at his agile best, because Liverpool overplayed Chelsea to the extent of making 39 scoring attempts — 28 of them on target. A week later, at home to Coventry, Bonetti made another penalty save.

October began with a 1-1 draw away to Queen's Park Rangers and, two days later, a one-nil defeat at Stoke in the League Cup. Not since 1967 had Chelsea failed first time in this competition.

In mid-October Stamford Bridge was saddened by the passing of one of the club's most beloved figures — Andy Wilson, who died aged 77 after a heart attack. His association with Chelsea had begun fifty years earlier, in November 1923, when he came to The Bridge from Middlesbrough, having previously played for Heart of Midlothian and Dunfermline.

Chelsea never had greater value for money than for the £6,000 they paid for Andy. At centre or inside-forward, he was a star of stars and one of the most artistic and creative footballers of his day. He played in 14 Internationals for Scotland, several times as captain, and in nine years with Chelsea (before moving to Q.P.R. in season 1931-32) he appeared in 238 League games and scored 59 goals.

Andy captained Chelsea back to the First Division in 1930, and when his playing, coaching and managerial days elsewhere were over he returned to London to work, to King's Road to live and to Stamford Bridge to follow the fortunes of his old club. Right to the end, Chelsea occupied a large part of his life and although, through failing health, he was unable to

Peter Bonetti caps a great performance at Liverpool with this penalty save from Kevin Keegan

A Chelsea milestone as Peter Osgood scores his 100th First Division goal at home to Everton in November

attend home games as often as he would have liked in the last few seasons, he relied on son Jimmy (who was himself on the playing staff here in the early post-war years) to keep him fully informed with first-hand accounts. Andy Wilson, a gentleman of Chelsea Football if ever there was one...

Chelsea finished October with a Friday night match at home to Norwich City – to avoid clashing with Q.P.R. v Arsenal the next day. The experiment did nothing for the gate (21,953), but the match produced the best form and most rewarding victory so far, by three clear goals which ended a run of five games for only two points. Tommy Baldwin snapped up two of them, giving him seven in eight League games, and this match marked the appearance of brothers in the side – 18-year-old Graham Wilkins at left-back and 17-year-old Ray ("Butch"), who went on as substitute when David Webb was injured. The Wilkins boys, from Hayes, Middlesex, are sons of former Brentford player George Wilkins, and they provided the third instance of brothers in Chelsea's first-team since the war. The others: the Silletts, Peter and John, and Ron and Allan Harris.

November was Chelsea's best month, both in results and performance. At Old Trafford a shot by Baldwin and a header by Osgood brought a 2-0 lead, and that was still the position with two minutes left, by which time thousands of disillusioned Manchester United fans had given up for the day and left the ground. But with a substitute on for the injured Garland, Chelsea were down to ten men for the last ten minutes after Graham Wilkins was carried off with a cracked fibula, and astonishingly United levelled the scores with goals by defenders Young and Greenhoff in the last 90 seconds.

The visit of Everton to Stamford Bridge on November 10 was a memorable occasion. On the morning of the match Osgood said: 'I got my 99th First Division goal last Saturday, and would love to reach the ton today in front of our own supporters.' He did, too, with an exquisite angled shot, added another for good measure in a 3-1 victory and, in celebration, blew kisses to the crowd. So Ossie joined four others – all England Internationals, like himself – in the club record book as scorers of a century of League goals for Chelsea: Bobby Tambling (164), Roy Bentley (128), Jimmy Greaves (124) and, pre-war, George Mills (116). Sir Alf Ramsey, present to see Osgood reach that milestone, gave him something more to celebrate by calling him back to the England team against Italy at Wembley four days later.

After a goalless draw at Highbury, Chelsea ended an

unbeaten November with their biggest score of the season, 4-0 at home to Southampton. This was another "special occasion", with Peter Bonetti becoming the first player in Chelsea history to reach 600 first-team appearances. He was made captain for the day and, at long distance, enjoyed the sight of Chelsea in full flow at the other end of the field. Ian Britton began the scoring (his first goal for the club), others came from Chris Garland and Steve Kember (2). It was so one-side that afterwards Southampton manager Laurie McMenemy said: 'I thought about appealing for bad light. There was no other way we could have stopped Chelsea today.'

By now Chelsea had climbed from the early-season doldrums almost to half-way. December's opening match, away to Stoke, was frozen off and then, at home to Leicester City, came a remarkable recovery from two down to win 3-2. The revival started just before half-time, when Hudson went down for a penalty which probably nine out of ten referees would not have given. Skipper John Hollins' spot-kick not only beat England goalkeeper Peter Shilton — it broke the net! Osgood equalised and, eight minutes from time, Hollins won the match with a second penalty.

Chelsea now had an unbeaten run of six matches behind them and were the second highest scorers in the First Division following successive home victories by 3-0, 3-1, 4-0 and 3-2. So they were in the form and the mood to receive Championship leaders Leeds United, whose objective in this particular match was to smash Liverpool's 19-game unbeaten record for the start of a season, set in 1949-50.

This fixture pulled the season's biggest crowd at Stamford Bridge (40,768), and they saw Chelsea make enough first-half chances to have settled the match. Right at the start Kember was through the middle but shot wide; Baldwin's close-in back-heel was smothered on the line by goalkeeper Harvey; Baldwin shot against a post and Garland miskicked in front of goal.

You pay for missed chances against teams like Leeds, as Chelsea discovered a minute before half-time. Bonetti, under pressure in the air, lost Bremner's corner from the right and Jordan scored with a fast hook. Ten minutes into the second half Osgood equalised with a superb header from Houseman's corner, but not for long were Chelsea level. Lorimer crossed deep to Jordan on the left...Jordon headed across and Jones hammered his shot past Bonetti for the winner.

In a sense, that moment, that shot, that match began the

break-up of what had appeared, over the previous half-dozen games the welcome prospect of a Chelsea team at last 'coming together.' Instead, it fell to pieces with a sequence of four defeats – against Leeds, Wolves (two-nil away) and two more home losses at Christmas, against West Ham and Liverpool.

The game against West Ham on a murky, misty Boxing Day morning was sheer pantomime. At half-time Chelsea led 2-0 against bottom-of-the-table opponents. West Ham had had hardly a kick, and looked certain of only one thing 1974 – the Second Division. Then, in eleven incredible minutes at the start of the second half, Chelsea went from two up to 2-3 down. At 2-1, just after Lampard's goal, Osgood, eight yards out, chested down Hollins' cross and was poised to make it 3-1. But his shot exploded against the crossbar...West Ham swept to the other end for Gould to equalise, and Clyde Best made the result 2-4 with two far-post headers from right-wing centres. Up to half-time Chelsea had decorated the Christmas tree with marvellous skills and movement, but at the finish the fairy on the top was wearing the claret and blue of West Ham.

The massive figure of Droy returned to the defence at home to Liverpool on December 29, with Hollins switching from the back four to his proper role of attacking midfield player. But after 22 minutes Toshack was as unmarked as West Ham's Best had been three days before, and his header for the only goal of the match meant that in a disastrous fortnight Chelsea had slumped to four defeats in a row – three of them at home.

With the start of the F.A. Cup only four days away, drastic changes were made away to Sheffield United on New Year's Day. Out went Bonetti, Hudson, Osgood and Baldwin, and although the new-look side won 2-1 Chelsea were heading for one of the most traumatic and troubled periods in their history.

Only forty-eight hours before the third round Cup-tie at home to Queen's Park Rangers, Osgood and Hudson refused to join the first-team squad for practice. The scene lasted only a few minutes and ended with the two 'rebels' driving away from Mitcham together. They were immediately suspended by the club, never to be seen again in first-team

Goodbye, Ossie. His last appearance for Chelsea at Stamford Bridge was two months before his transfer to Southampton – in the Reserves at home to Ipswich on January 12. It lasted only 18 minutes; then he injured a groin and was helped to the dressing-room by Combination trainer Reg Byatt

competition for Chelsea, whose statement on the blow-up said briefly: 'Alan Hudson and Peter Osgood refused to train with the first-team squad this morning, for which they are being suspended for one week. Both players expressed a wish to move, and Chelsea are making them available for transfer as from now.'

There was desperation all over Chelsea's play in the 0-0 draw with Rangers, and the tie would have been over first time had not Phillips anticipated the direction of Francis's penalty and also made other magnificent saves from Bowles and Leach. If Bonetti's long reign was over, here surely was a worthy successor between the posts for Chelsea.

Meanwhile, there was no shortage of predicted destinations for Osgood in the newspapers — Real Madrid, Manchester United, Derby County, Stoke, Tottenham and Crystal Palace were all named on the kites flown, but never a mention of Southampton at this stage. But if Osgood commanded constant headlines and speculation, the transfer of Hudson went through first — to Stoke for some £240,000 on Saturday, January 12. That same morning Osgood turned down a move to Derby; in the afternoon he turned out in the

reserves at home to Ipswich, and limped off with a groin injury after 18 minutes....the last time he was to be seen in Chelsea blue on the Stamford Bridge pitch.

Three days later, in a mud-marred replay which had been twice postponed because of the waterlogged ground, Chelsea went out of the Cup to Bowles' header for Rangers – their first third round exit since 1962, and the first time ever that Chelsea had failed to score in both League and F.A. Cups in the same season.

There was a surprise signing within 48 hours. Dave Sexton bought back Charlie Cooke from Crystal Palace for £17,000 sixteen months after he left Stamford Bridge for Selhurst Park for £85,000. Said Chelsea's manager: 'Charlie is coming back to do a special job, to give us more mobility on the wings. We are getting back a highly experienced player, a player we all know and who knows us, and one who is popular within the club and with our fans. There is no sentiment about this – it is a calculated decision. It's simply that, in the present circumstances, with a lot of young players in the team, I believe Charlie can make a really positive contribution to Chelsea's football. He will operate as an orthodox winger, bringing width to the attack and releasing Chris Garland into the centre, where he is happiest and most effective.' And Charlie, 'rescued' at 31 from reserve football with a club at the bottom of the Second Division, showed as he made his second Chelsea debut in the 1-1 draw at home to Derby that the hips still swayed and the feet still twinkled.

But the Osgood situation hung more oppressively than ever over Stamford Bridge, and the club programme for the match against Derby brought the issue into the open for the first time with this editorial: 'Recent events at Stamford Bridge have caused us all anxiety and great distress, for unity of feeling within the Club at all levels is something on which we have long prided ourselves. In the formation of a football club, particularly the team itself, skill, flair, dedication and loyalty are vital ingredients but, as with any organisation, we depend most of all on human personal relationships. Of these, the relationship between Manager and Playing Staff is an absolute prerequisite for the ultimate success and happiness of a club.

'But there comes a time in everyone's life – at work, within families, in sport – when there is a clash of personalities, and it is evident that for some time such a

The end of Chelsea's Cup hopes. Q.P.R.'s Stan Bowles (in front of goalpost) heads the only goal of the FA Cup third round replay at Shepherds Bush

situation has existed at Stamford Bridge between Manager and one or two Players. Occasional rifts are part of the internal life of every club. When they have happened at Chelsea, every effort has always been made to breach such rifts, as indeed was done in this case. But, since Peter Osgood and Alan Hudson were insistent that the situation could not be improved, the Board felt they had no alternative but to make them available for transfer. In so doing – and obviously we part with players of their talent with great reluctance – we would like to thank them for their services to Chelsea and wish them success in the future.

'Our principal emotion is one of distress and disappointment that these events should have happened, but in taking of all major decisions the long-term future and good of our Club must come above all other considerations. We have backed Manager Dave Sexton 100 per cent in this matter and believe that, with the same backing from our Players, Staff and Supporters, we shall be able to look back on recent happenings, unhappy though they have been, as a point in Chelsea history from which we grew in stature.'

Back on the field, the month ended with Chelsea visiting Stoke in a re-arranged game on January 27 – the first Sunday fixture ever staged in the First Division. Not unexpectedly, Alan Hudson turned on the style for his new club against the old, and it was his sprawl in the penalty-area that brought Stoke an arguable penalty and the only goal of the game.

February opened with an impressive performance at Leeds, where Bill Garner's header earned at 1-1 draw on a ground where Chelsea have not won in the League since August 1936. This was followed by a 1-0 victory at home to Manchester City and draws against Q.P.R. (3-3 at home) and at Ipswich (1-1).

Osgood, meantime, had recovered from groin trouble and, on February 16, made what was to be his final appearance for Chelsea five hundred miles away in a friendly which was lost 1-2 at Aberdeen. Still the question in many minds was whether manager and player might yet settle their personal differences, but suddenly came the showdown. Board meetings at Stamford Bridge are normally held once a month

Whose back...or who's back?
Charlie Cooke, of course, on his return from Crystal Palace
Complete with boots and ready to play again for Chelsea

Welcome home, Charlie!

AM & WILKINSON
Tel. CONGLETON
PICCADILLY-HANLEY

on Wednesdays, so there was an air of 'something special' about that called for Monday, March 4, two days after Chelsea's 0-3 collapse at West Ham had sent them to within one place of the three relegation positions in the First Division.

The headlines that night blared SEXTON LEAVES CHELSEA and, indeed, all the signs were that Dave Sexton had decided to end his 6½-year reign at Stamford Bridge. For he had left the ground early in the afternoon, telling several players as he went that he was leaving the club, thanking them for their efforts under him and wishing them good luck in the future.

Chairman Brian Mears insisted that there had been a misunderstanding, and so it proved. Next day Dave Sexton explained: 'I misunderstood something that was said at the board meeting – something to do with Osgood – and left under the impression that the club wanted me to go. I was wrong, as a telephone call from the chairman made clear later that evening. I knew then that I was still manager of Chelsea. I was not asked to resign. I did not offer to resign, and have no intention of doing so. People are naturally anxious about our position in the First Division table, and we realise that we are too close to the bottom for comfort. In view of our position at the moment, it is essential that we have stability. That's why I must choose players I know I can rely on.'

Dave Sexton had battled through the most critical 24 hours of his career. Nine days later, the day before the season's deadline for moves, Osgood was transferred to Southampton for £275,000. That same Wednesday afternoon, at home to Burnley in a re-arranged match, and watched by the smallest post-war League crowd at Stamford Bridge (8,171), Chelsea won 3-0 and rose seven places in the table. If ever they needed to win, it was on the day Peter Osgood, the previous season's Player of the Year at Chelsea, left the club. This was the end of one era, the start of another.

Alan Hudson and Peter Osgood on opposite sides in the First Division and neither wearing a Chelsea shirt. At the start of last season this would have seemed an 'impossible' picture, but it was real enough in March, when Osgood made his Southampton debut away to Stoke. The signing of Hudson lifted Stoke, but Ossie found himself in a relegation fight with the Saints

There **was** something to smile about at the Bridge last season — John Hollins points out the four stitches David Webb needed over the right eye after the match at Coventry

THINGS THEY SAID IN 1973-74

HARRY MEDHURST, as he handed over the position of head trainer to son Norman at the start of the season and became Chelsea's physiotherapist: 'Every second counts when a player is injured. It is vital to get out there quickly and, because of an arthritic knee, I can no longer do that. I shall miss those moments and the deep involvement with the team on match-days, but I am delighted to be carrying on as physio and hope to do so for several years.'

STEVE KEMBER, talking about goalscoring on the eve of the season: 'My goal totals have been going down – four, three and two in the past three seasons. The reason? I was getting into positions, but not putting the ball away. I mean to do something about it in 1973-74.'

PETER BONETTI, on his historic 600th first-team appearance for Chelsea at home to Southampton on November 24: 'After the worst winter of my career, when I was out injured for five months, I am grateful to have come back to fitness and form. Many people said I was finished, and it gives me a lot of satisfaction to have proved them wrong. I've no idea how long I am likely to go on playing. I would like to think I will carry on and clock up seven hundred games – but if the reflexes go before then I shall know when it is time to pack up.'

DAVE SEXTON, on the rise of Gary Locke: 'I remember very well the youth cup-tie which convinced me that full-back was going to be Gary's role. Until that particular match he had played midfield from the time he joined Chelsea as a schoolboy. Then Ken Shellito, our Youth manager, tried a

BILL GARNER – 'The secret of heading is getting up early and hanging there'

MICKY DROY – 'There are not many forwards about of my size....'

switch. I was sitting with Ken, and we saw the winger push the ball past Gary on the outside and run him. Gary kept with him, waiting for just the right moment to slide into the tackle. I turned to Ken and said 'That's the nearest thing to you I've seen.' Ken was very difficult to pass on the line, and Gary reminded me of him so much that I thought here was a player for the future at right-back.'

BILL GARNER, on heading: 'The secret is getting up early and hanging there. I've always had that ability. It also helps to know which defences struggle on crosses to the far post — that's why I like to do my homework, watching as many matches as I can on TV.'

CHAIRMAN BRIAN MEARS, on the controversial subject of football on television: 'I don't want to see soccer taken off the screens — I believe it can help the game considerably. But the TV people should understand our difficulties and realise that their present coverage of the game is not always helpful. For example, they show film shots of spectacular action in Saturday preview programmes at a time when people would normally be leaving home for the soccer grounds. I would far rather see them use their football films and interviews to make people aware of soccer's attractions much earlier. Friday night is the ideal time.'

DAVE SEXTON, before the home game against Leeds on December 15: 'We are playing attractively and well now, and banging in the goals. Our new stand is taking shape, and the ground is beginning to feel alive again. We are over the hill with that and with our injury problems, and I have not been so confident about the future of Chelsea for a long time.'

DAVID WEBB, before the same match: 'Playing Leeds is often a turning point for us. A few years ago they beat us 5 - 2 at The Bridge, but we went on to beat them in the Cup Final. Last season it was the other way round — we beat them 4 - 0 here on the opening day and hardly won another home game all year. But when we were struggling later in the season, we went up to Leeds and drew 1 - 1. That got us going again.'

DAVID WEBB, after Leeds' 2 - 1 win at Stamford Bridge: 'This was Bremner's day. He was Leeds. Bremner was the man. He came at us for ninety minutes non-stop. The big factor was always Bremner. They ought to make a special championship trophy for him. Make no mistake, when

Bremner goes Leeds have their first real crisis. I believe he has done as much for that club as Don Revie.'

MICKY DROY, on 'arriving' in the First Division: 'There are not many forwards about of my size (6ft. 4½in.), so I ought to win most balls in the air, and I'm big enough to carry my weight (15st.) without feeling that it slows me down. As a schoolboy I trained with my local club, Arsenal — I played in the same Islington Schools team as Charlie George — but I did not get on there, so stopped going. After leaving school I played for several amateur clubs, Hoddesdon Town, Wembley and Slough Town. I did jobs like labouring, floor-laying and cold storage work at Smithfield meat market. I started to do well at Slough under manager Tommy Lawrence. Spurs and Portsmouth looked at me, but I chose Chelsea because the set-up seemed best here.'

CHRIS GARLAND, discussing the matter of goalkeepers moving before a penalty-kick is taken: 'I think it is more or less accepted that all 'keepers move a fraction before the ball is struck. I don't blame referees; after all, it's impossible to watch two players twelve yards apart simultaneously. The solution is simple — be good at the penalty-taking job and it doesn't matter then if the 'keeper does move.'

IAN HUTCHINSON — 'Sometimes I wonder about all this "brave Hutch" talk'

JOHN HOLLINS — 'The hardest goal to get is the third...'

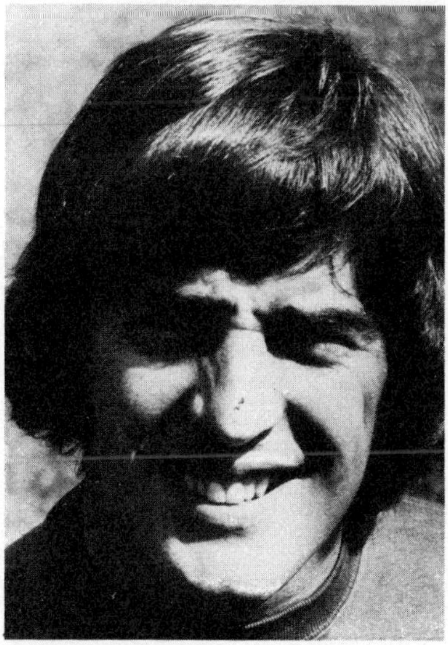

IAN HUTCHINSON, during his continued fight for fitness: 'I've stopped worrying about my injuries. They are all behind me, and there is not much point in talking about bad luck. I just have to buckle down and get 100 per cent fit. The main problem is weight put on during the last lay-off, but I'll soon run that off in training. Sometimes I wonder about all this 'brave Hutch' talk. You play the way you are made. If you try to change, you lose a lot of your natural ability.'

BILL SHANKLY, Liverpool manager, on Hutchinson's comeback: 'I am delighted to hear that Chelsea's Ian Hutchinson is playing again. He has been so desperately unlucky with injuries over these past three years, and I sincerely hope he makes a complete recovery this time. Hutchinson is a big, brave lad who has skill as well as courage – the type of bustling striker who is a rare commodity these days. He also has the longest throw-in I have ever seen. My eyes nearly popped out of my head the first time I saw Ian play for Chelsea against Liverpool and he threw the ball to the far post. Good luck, son. I hope to see you playing for Chelsea against Liverpool again soon...even if those big throw-ins are a confounded nuisance!'

DAVE SEXTON, on dedication: 'Perhaps it's a flaw in me, but I can't believe a player is anything less than dedicated. It's always a terrible shock when it's proved otherwise. I don't understand that Friday night out business. A player's career is so short that I can't understand how one can throw away his talent, the honours, the money he can earn, the pleasure he can take from playing. Yet some do. Perhaps they are unlucky in their friends.'

JOHN HOLLINS, on the 'problem' of leading two-nil: 'The hardest goal to get is the third when you are two up. Not many teams come back from three down – although it has been done, by Chelsea among them – but at two down you are still there with a chance. You've only got to pull one back and you say to yourselves 'one more and we're level.' We've seen it happen both ways at The Bridge this season – we beat Leicester 3-2 from two down, and we lost 4-2 to West Ham after leading two-nil.'

DON REVIE, Leeds United manager, commenting on the Osgood – Hudson transfer situation: 'A manager of a big London club should be paid about £2,000 more than his counterparts in other towns or cities. That is a measure of how difficult I believe managing a club can be in London, where the players are subjected to pressures which can ruin their dedication to the game. Leading London players are inundated with enough social and business offers to keep them fully occupied every day of the week, and it is never easy for them to know when to draw the line. Chelsea epitomize this type of problem, as they are situated in one of London's most fashionable districts – the ground is a free-kick away from the 'swinging' Kings Road – and they have a tremendous following among show business personalities. Their players have a trendy, glamorous image, and the hangers-on are attracted to them like bees to a honeypot. You can be certain that Dave Sexton did not really want to let such gifted players as Hudson and Osgood go but, in the circumstances, he had little option.'

DAVID WEBB, on the men who will safeguard football's future: 'I'm firmly of the view that the game suffered in this country through England winning the World Cup in 1966 and creating a monument at which too many worshipped without question. But with equal conviction, I believe that football will save itself because there are so many personalities in the game strong enough to throw the lifebelt. They are young men I bracket in the 'new manager' generation. They are not managers yet, and many of them are still playing in the top class – like Frank McLintock and Terry Venables. They are intelligent individuals who will not strangle the individual's rights on the field and will not try to blind you with over-indulged talking on the game. They will know the good player when they see one, and they will encourage him to play his way and as best it suits the team.'

BRIAN MEARS, discussing Chelsea's needs at the gate: 'We cannot contemplate an average crowd of less than 30,000. Our redevelopment plans are based on the optimistic belief that Chelsea will be successful.'

GARY LOCKE, on attacking out of defence: 'I know defence is basically my job, but I get a terrific kick out of making goals, too. I get really excited when I see one of my crosses knocked into the net. It's not only a boost for me, but good for the whole team because goals are what we are all playing for.'

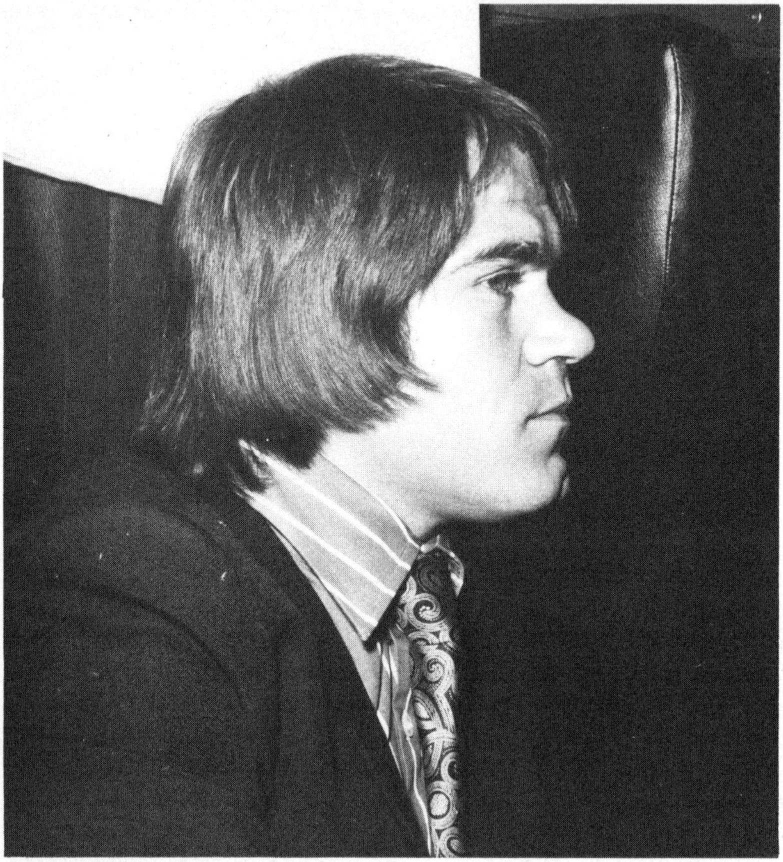

DAVID WEBB — 'I believe the game here suffered through England winning the World Cup'

CHARLIE COOKE, after his Chelsea 'homecoming' match against Derby County: 'I hadn't had a full game for three weeks and thought I might run out of puff, but by the end I wanted to go on for another 45 minutes. The Chelsea crowd were special. They've always loved me. At Crystal Palace, if I played brilliantly — which wasn't often — they just about let me get away with it. There were days over there when I wanted to throw my shirt at one of them and tell them to get on with it. But at Stamford Bridge they would clap me just for standing up in a strong wind. That makes you want to do the business for them in return, but I hope they don't expect too much for seventeen grand! I must admit I thought my First Division days were over and that I'd be finishing my career with a little club. It came as a real surprise, a pleasant shocker, when I heard Chelsea were in for me. Not many players get the chance to make this sort of move so late in a career — to be so much a part of Chelsea, move on and then come back again. I'm going to try to play the way I did in my two or three great seasons here. I know that's what the crowd want as well. Some people may doubt me coming back, but I believe I can live up to what is required and entertain the show business element at Chelsea for four more years. I've got to. I've dropped money to come back. Dave Sexton is a hard dealer who's made sure I've got to hold onto a first-team place to keep up my standard of living.'

DAVID WEBB, needing three stitches over the left eye at Leeds just after four over the other eye away to Coventry: 'That's about forty stitches I've had in my head during my career. I'm the Henry Cooper of football...but I've never been stopped yet. It's getting worse for us defenders. You get forwards challenging for balls they've no right to get to. Managers are geeing them up all the time. The defender is just about to head the ball when the forward tries to back-head it. You catch the back of his head in your face...and it's you who needs the embroidery.'

GARY LOCKE — 'I get a terrific kick out of making goals'

CHARLIE COOKE — 'The fans at Stamford Bridge have always loved me — they'd clap me just for standing up in a strong wind '

DAVID SEXTON, on the final break with Peter Osgood: 'Ossie has done a lot of good things for Chelsea, won us many a game, but it is not something you can list like a balance sheet. I'm sorry the situation has cropped up again. I don't like tearing anything apart. The whole business of being a manager is to put things together. My entire thinking is based on that principle — building, not destroying. It's simply that there comes a time when you have to act the way you feel is right, regardless of whether it's popular or not. This is a horrific period for me. Managing and coaching is all about unison. The hard core of our club is entirely together and getting on with the job. But there has been some splintering, and that makes me unhappy. We know the heart

of this club is still absolutely sound, but people outside must be wondering what the hell is going on. They must think we are in a right old mess. What we need now is a little privacy so that we can get on with the fight against the pressure we're under in the League. We're scrapping away...we think we can do the job...but we don't need any extra problems.'
BILL GARNER, after the transfer-listing of Peter Osgood: 'I don't want to be looked on as the man who has taken over Chelsea's No.9 shirt from Ossie. That's why I am still wearing No.10 and Steve Kember is playing midfield in the nine shirt. Since I came to Chelsea, I have been playing left-side, whereas before I had always been a target man in the centre. I believe that's my best position, but if I'm asked to do another job because it means a first-team place, I'm happy to do so.'
BRIAN MEARS, on the future of football: 'No factor is more important than providing comfortable facilities for spectators. That is why Chelsea embarked on a £5½ million redevelopment programme. We believe, long-term, that more people will support us if they can come here as family units. Some supporters have been fearful of taking wives and children to matches, but fortunately hooliganism is on the decrease. Making grounds attractive and inviting must be an important part of the drive to bring back our soccer prosperity. Football's great priority is to win back the crowds. One way to do this is by providing the kind of attacking football people want to watch. We do not need a complex new system of points scoring. Goals will come if more clubs adopt positive methods. Maybe we do play too much football. Maybe the Football League does need streamlining. But careful thought is needed, and people in the game should gather round a table far more often. We still have a wonderful product. If it is sold right – and that has to happen – the game cannot fail to attract.'
DAVE SEXTON, on Chelsea's future: Each season is like a woman having a baby. It is nine months long, and you're sure what you are going to get at the end. Some have nice babies...like winning the Cup. Our baby just now is the stand. It's a bit of a jumbo, and we've had problems with delivery. The stand has been a helluva burden to carry, because the club has gone out on a limb, and everything depends on the playing side for its success. We've had difficult times before and come through, and I am confident we shall do so again.'

STAMFORD BRIDGE IN 1980

John Moynihan (Sunday Telegraph)

There were times just after the war when the prospect of Chelsea Football Club winning any prizes remained as remote as running into a Martian on Parsons Green. Slavish allegiance to the 'Pensioners' on my part usually meant trooping down the Fulham Road on misty days to watch our beloved team playing well and losing or playing badly and winning. Such erratic performances hardly suggested a successful time was round the corner.

If, say in 1951, after Chelsea had avoided relegation by .044 of a goal, a fellow supporter on the terraces had suggested our team would be Football League Champions in four years, I would have assumed he was either suffering from a touch of the sun or a loose screw. But Chelsea did actually climb off the floor and win the Championship in their golden jubilee year, thus proving that any forecasts about the future of the Blues must be approached with grave caution.

In attempting to forecast Chelsea's prospects for 1980, I know I am entering a dangerous and mysterious maze. It might be easier just to say the Walrus and the Carpenter will form the right-wing then — and simply leave it at that. Being realistic may land me in the same trouble as many other amateur clairvoyants on the subject of Chelsea's future.

Still, Dave Sexton, who has always been cautious about predicting results did tip Chelsea as the F.A. Cup-winning side in 1970, so I will accept the challenge with optimism, hoping one of the most unpredictable teams in history will not let me down.

Before the futuristic part, however, let us return to times when it was unsafe to say anything about Chelsea without being proved wrong. One of the first Chelsea clairvoyants who knew he wasn't giving the wrong answer was tubby goalkeeper Bill Foulke before the first competitive match the club ever played on September 2nd, 1905. The match was away to Stockport County in the Second Division, and the representatives of Stamford Bridge had to walk from the local station to the ground as was the custom in those harsh

Chairman Brian Mears (left) and secretary Tony Green look down on Stamford Bridge from a great height — from the top of the new East Stand before the roof went on last season

days. Foulke, weighing twenty stone and six foot three inches tall, was accosted by a tiny Lancashire lad who fired an insolent verbal dart at the giant: 'Ye'll get licked today.' Foulke looked down at the midget and answered benevolently: 'Then it'll be for the first time, me lad.'

Foulke was right. Chelsea lost that day through a solo penalty goal, but it took them only two seasons to win promotion to the First Division. I caught up with them many decades later shortly after they played their famous match against Moscow Dynamo at Stamford Bridge in November 1945. Tommy Lawton was our hero in those early post-war days. The old Shed was full of ex-soldiers wearing brown trilbies and demob macs, and they used to predict unwisely that, with Tom heading so many goals off his Brylcreamed head the Cup would be won by the following spring. But the Cup was to elude us for another 25 years or so — although we would have scoffed at the thought then.

My schoolmates said I was always too optimistic about Chelsea's future. Usually they were right. The Chelsea forwards often thought the Shed was a better place to boot the ball than the opposing net — particularly a rugged winger dear to our hearts called Benny Jones, blessed with a left foot as lethal as Tosh Chamberlain's later at Fulham.

Tom Lawton had been transferred to Notts County in 1947 — a move he subsequently bitterly regretted — and a new hero came on the scene, Roy Bentley from Newcastle. But Chelsea continued to infuriate with their fickle play. After one match I wrote in my scrapbook: 'Chelsea played like champions against Portsmouth in the first half but after the change over, they played like a local works team and lost.'

Ken Armstrong, captain John Harris, goalkeeper Harry Medhurst, Bobby Campbell, Tommy Walker and Bentley all participated in those carefree times when nobody knew just what the side would do from one week to the next. My cuttings of the period include headlines reflecting the club's wayward existence: CHELSEA IN LOW GEAR is followed the next week by CHELSEA'S NEW LOOK MADE ARSENAL LOOK RAGGED.

We youngsters in the Shed all had our own views on what was wrong with Chelsea. There were many remedies suggested, like buying a completely new team. One tiny supporter called Shorty, who was only five foot three tall, said he liked coming to Stamford Bridge because although he hardly saw a ball kicked, he new he had 'not missed much'. I wrote a frustrated letter about Chelsea to a National newspaper and they actually printed it: 'The trouble with Chelsea, at the moment, is their habit of playing beautiful football up to the penalty-area and then almost casting lots to decide who should take the final shot.'

Then things got better, Roy Bentley started hitting the net and we began predicting Chelsea would at last reach a Wembley final. This proved incorrect, but only just. The idea seemed beautifully real — for half an hour at White Hart

Gary Locke, full-back with a great future. Chelsea's Player of the Year 1974 was, at 19, the youngest ever to win the award

John Hollins — driving Chelsea on towards the Eighties

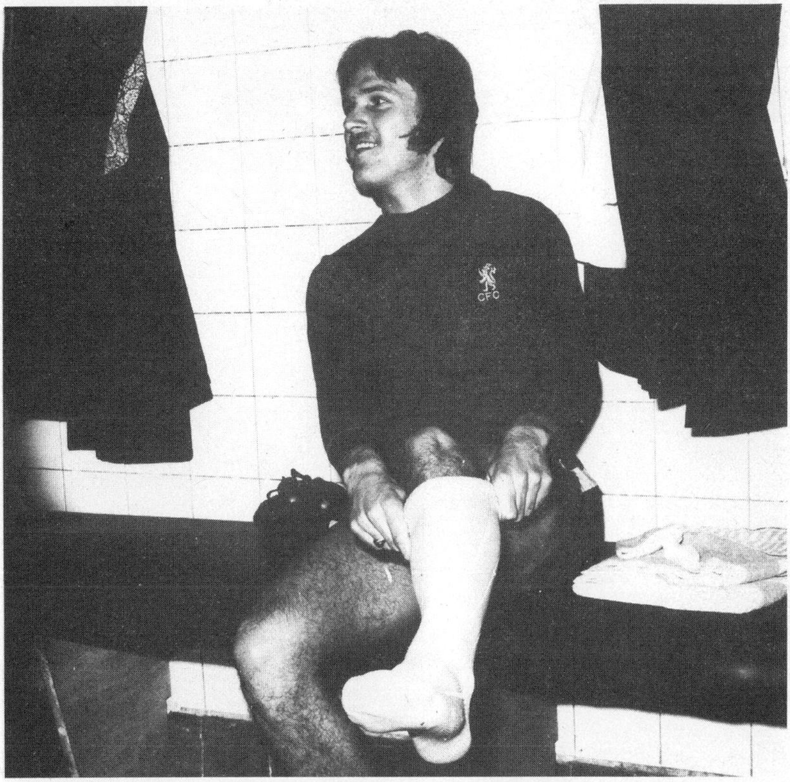

Lane in 1950 in a pulsating semi-final against Arsenal. Two goals up through Bentley, the Chelsea contingent bellowing their heads off, my blue and white scarf soaked with perspiration – we were surely there. But then Freddie Cox, direct from a corner, and Leslie Compton in the second half ruined the canvas. Suddenly Arsenal were in command and Denis Compton, as he reminded me only the other day, hit the crossbar with a diving header. I didn't have to be reminded. The memory was as clear as today.

Chelsea still seemed to have enough talent and teamwork to win the replay but it was Cox who knocked one past Harry Medhurst in extra time. Chelsea had to wait another seventeen years for Wembley – although they reached three more semi-finals – again losing against Arsenal in 1952 after another replay, and being edged out by Liverpool and Sheffield Wednesday in 1965 and 1966.

There were still times when it was difficult to forecast just what the Blues were going to do. In 1955, they burst through in the run-up to win their first Championship, urged on by some strong dashes by a favourite 'Rabbit' of the wing, Eric Parsons, and more fine goals by Bentley. Peter Sillett's thundering penalty-kick, which won the vital Easter match against runners-up Wolves, was enough to make us feel that Chelsea would lead the world for years. But all too soon they became their erratic selves and slipped down the table the following season.

Now from the hidden pens of youth football came a young genius called Jimmy Greaves. If only I could predict Chelsea will be blessed with another like him by 1980. But impossible; he was unique, a phenomenal and natural goal-scorer. When he first played in the first team at Stamford Bridge, he looked so skinny in his long Alex James shorts that the very idea of his actually surviving a match without being blown away in the wind seemed remote. But once Jimmy went zipping through on one of those long dashes down the centre, the ball would stick and stick to his feet until it had been planted firmly in the net. Ask Billy Wright!

Flashback (1): Tommy Lawton, Chelseas's first big signing after the war

Flashback (2): Roy Bentley, star marksman of the Fifties and captain of Chelsea's Championship-winning team of 20 years ago

Flashback (3): Jimmy Greaves in typical shooting action for Chelsea, at home to Spurs in April 1961

One goal among the hundreds Greaves scored for England, Chelsea and Spurs remains in the memory — a whirling turn on the edge of the box at The Bridge in a match against Preston, followed by a withering shot past Else. The goalkeeper stood there applauding as the leather cooled off in the netting.

How Jimmy would grace the new streamlined Stamford Bridge arena! But while he lives across London in prosperous football retirement, the game seems generally barren of magicians of his kind.

When he was at Chelsea, we predicted a whole list of honours for the club, but despite his century on the goalscoring front, the team seldom prospered. When Greaves left for A.C. Milan in 1961, and Chelsea went down a year later to the Second Division, it would have taken a courageous punter to forecast what a splendid team they would become under Tommy Docherty only two or three years later after returning to Division 1. My own special memory of that era is the F.A. Cup defeat of the Cup-holders Liverpool at dreaded Anfield in 1966 in the third round. The same team-spirit and confidence showed by the Blues that day will, I trust, be ever on the boil in the 1980 side.

Bobby Tambling's goal, which followed Peter Osgood's header and sealed the 2 - 1 victory, was one of the classic moves in Chelsea's history — a fine save by Peter Bonetti, a quick throw to Terry Venables, on to Ron Harris, to Tambling, and then out to George Graham on the right wing. A perfect centre and Tambling was waiting to head the ball in. Not one sturdy Liverpool player had touched the ball.

The same spirit prevailed, of course, when Chelsea won the F.A. Cup at last in 1970 and the European Cup-Winners' Cup a year later. That refusal to surrender against Leeds in the replay at Old Trafford which led to Osgood and Dave Webb scoring the vital goals would inspire a Chelsea side in 1980 as it did in 1970.

So what can we expect as Chelsea move towards their 75th birthday? As far as the playing structure of English League

We've had many a Chelsea player capped, and now we've got them helmeted as the first-ream squad turn up on the East Stand building site. After two years of match-day silence on that side of the stadium, they will be glad to have support from all round Stamford Bridge again in 1974-75

Chelsea's long-term future is in the hands — and feet — of talented teenagers like these. Back row, left to right: Brian Bason, Ray ("Butch") Wilkins, Ian Britton. Front row: Mike Brolly, Gary Locke, Garry Stanley

12
12

23
29
15
23
29
15

football is concerned, some sort of major revision is needed to streamline an overloaded fraternity. A move to trim the Scottish Leagues recently will, I feel, almost certainly be followed in England before the 1980s. The First Division, in particular, could be trimmed down to fifteen or so clubs. Better still, as a firm believer in a super-league for the cream of European clubs, I would like to see teams like Ajax of Amsterdam, Juventus of Turin, A.C. Milan and Inter, C.F. Barcelona, Real Madrid and Bayern Munich playing at the 'new' Bridge. After all, with a supersonic plane like a Concorde available, it would take only a matter of minutes to fly the Ajax players from Amsterdam to London.

The era when English spectators regarded foreign teams and players as clowns passed years ago thanks to television, and there would be huge support to see players like Johan Cruyff, Franz Beckenbauer and Gunter Netzer playing here regularly against teams like Leeds, Liverpool, Arsenal, Spurs and, naturally, Chelsea.

I also believe the recruitment of top foreign stars would do our domestic football no harm at all – though it would probably take far longer than 1980 to see a Cruyff or Beckenbauer trotting out on the Stamford Bridge turf as a Chelsea player. We British are still governed by a stretch of water between Dover and Calais and are less ready to accept foreigners on a regular player basis than the Italians or Spaniards. But Cruyff, for one, has really inspired Barcelona since his transfer from Ajax for nearly £1 million.

In the meantime, Chelsea do have a number of highly promising home products who should be experienced members of the team at the end of this decade. Two years before Chelsea's 75th birthday, the 1978 World Cup will take place in Argentina, where I feel England will be on show again and surely equipped with at least one Chelsea player.

That player, the crystal ball tells me, will be Gary Locke, a right-back with talents already rivalling those of gifted Chelsea full-backs of other days like Tommy Law, Ken Shellito and Eddie McCreadie.

Towering centre-back Micky Droy improved enormously last season and could establish himself as another Stan Wicks, Chelsea's centre-half in the 1955 Championship side. Droy still shows areas of inconsistency; for example, in a League match against Queen's Park Rangers here last February, he made a goal for Charlie Cooke and a minute or two later gave a free scoring gift to Stan Bowles while dreaming about his 'assist'.

Chelsea's dream home of the future...but when will it become reality? For if the new East Stand took two years to build instead of one as scheduled (and its cost went up from £1½ to £2 million), can the whole redevelopment project at Stamford Bridge be completed by the end of the Seventies, the original target? Only time — and money — will tell

These two, I hope, will be around in 1980 and I have a feeling John Hollins will still be master-minding the centre of operations like Sir Francis Drake. Another promising player, Ian Britton may have grown an inch or two by then and added a pound or two — and with football moving more towards a resurrection of wingers, his contribution could be as valuable to Chelsea as that of Eric Parsons back in the fifties.

Wingers, to the connoisseur, are the essence of the game: Matthews, Finney, Garrincha, Gento, Best — what would football have done without them? So I hope Chelsea's 1980 formation — and indeed the majority of our top English clubs — will have made their services less obsolete by the end of the decade.

Tactics must surely veer more and more towards attractive, attacking 'total' football inspired so successfully by Ajax and West Germany. The allegiance to defensive football taken up by English clubs since the 1966 World Cup win, which resulted in the ultimate horror of 4-4-2, will have faded away by the 1980s, if only to woo back spectators.

All good teams must have an 'entertainer' and Charlie Cooke's return to Stamford Bridge, after a brief stay at Crystal Palace, was a highly popular move. The uncanny ball skills, the shrewd passes, the loitering runs were back again. If not from Charlie, such arts, I hope, will be coming from some other individual within the team framework to keep Chelsea's ticket-office working overtime into the eighties.

Stamford Bridge will obviously be a Utopian bowl by then – the players will be even faster and fitter than they are now, the crowds even more fastidious. Sponsorship may have become more and more the lifeblood of football – but I would hate to see the Blues running around advertising sponsors on their chests as they do in France.

Chelsea's new stadium by 1980 should provide a recreational and social centre for players and fans alike. But football will remain paramount. I do not think the craze for Sunday football will stay with us – the players themselves want one day at least to take their families out or relax away from the pressures. Saturday will still be top soccer day in 1980.

And how will the Blues do in the years between? That is a riddle which must obviously, in view of previous disappointments, be approached with grave caution. The League Championship – or a new European Super League – may take rather longer to claim than five years. But somewhere nearer on the blue horizon, I can see the twin towers of Wembley welcoming the Chelsea lads again. Remember to check this coupon in 1980!

Dave Sexton poses the question: SUNDAY AT THE BRIDGE?

Sunday football became the big new talking point last season, when soccer on the seventh day was played for the first time by a good many League clubs between January and March. The situation was brought about by the industrial crisis that hit Britain in December, and Football League clubs – left to make up their own minds – took extreme views. It was a case of 'never on Sunday' or 'perhaps.'

Chelsea saw no reason to put on Sunday football at Stamford Bridge. The board kept an open mind on the subject, and we showed our willingness to take part in the general experiment by playing Stoke City away on Sunday, January 27, when a crowd of nearly 32,000 certainly indicated enthusiasm for the idea in and around the Potteries.

I know that in a programme poll, Chelsea supporters voted heavily against Sunday football being staged at The Bridge. But exactly how accurately that reflected **everyone's** opinion was in some doubt because it seemed that the majority of those who wrote in on the subject were long-time followers of Chelsea rather than teenage fans, who are potentially our long-term supporters of the future. And, obviously, younger fans are much more amenable to changes in tradition.

None of the other London First Division clubs, Arsenal, Queen's Park Rangers, Tottenham and West Ham, played Sunday matches last winter so, at top level, the experiment remained unproven in the capital city. But I believe that in time to come we may well find that Sunday does become a football day – yes, even at Stamford Bridge.

As a Common Market country, Britain is closer to Europe than ever before – and this is likely to bring us closer to the Continental-type Sunday, too. Remember also that London has more counter-attractions on Saturday afternoon than anywhere else in this country. They are not only other sports and leisure pursuits either; the football played by other clubs in and around London can lure many fans away – particularly the 'floaters' who choose their matches as

Relaxed and smiling on the training ground...deep in concentration in the trainer's box on match-day. The constrasting moods of modern football management as depicted by Dave Sexton.

supporters of football rather than avid followers of a particular team.

Chelsea, as you know, are in the middle of a complete facelift at Stamford Bridge. The 'new' stadium promises to be as futuristic as it is possible to be, and our enterprising board of directors have incorporated in these plans practically all the suggestions ever made for making the football ground a place for the family – modern stands, much more seating and covered accommodation, restaurant and bars, a covered concourse linking the stadium direct to Fulham Broadway station, private boxes.

In view of these far-reaching changes, it is my personal view that Sunday football could be the thing to pack our ground, because the game's future, I feel, lies in family participation. Now that the ordinary working man has so much time for leisure, he is looking for ways to involve his family in his favourite sport. It is up to the clubs to provide facilities that will attract.

When Stamford Bridge is rebuilt, we will have a vast number of seats – seats which have got to be filled if our capital outlay is not to be in vain. I do not want to see British football grounds become entirely seated, because there will always be a large number of people who prefer to stand. But if we can strike a balance between seating and standing, and a balance between attracting families and playing the game on a Sunday, then it is surely going to be beneficial for the future of the game.

Family-rate season-tickets will need to be considered, and I can see a definite future for private boxes available to business people. What better than to wine and dine their clients in the Stamford Bridge restaurant at lunchtime on Saturday, and then enjoy a luxury view of, say, Chelsea versus Liverpool?

What nobody can say is how successful we are going to be on the field in our new-look home at Stamford Bridge. Success in football is an intangible quality, because no matter how hard you work for it no-one can guarantee that you will actually win something big. So the pressures on me as manager, and on the players, to bring further success to Chelsea are therefore greater now than ever before.

Following England's exit from the World Cup last year, football was riddled with suggestions for change in the structure of the game, and the loudest cry was for an alteration to the offside law. But would this bring back the fans? I do not think so. What it would do is make the game easier and less competitive. Fans all over the country still want to see football fought out keenly under existing tried and tested legislation. And, after all, not many First Division teams employ offside traps these days.

Skill is what the game is all about and, restrictive offside rules or not, it will always be the teams with skill and invention who ultimately succeed. I have never heard many strong suggestions for widening the goals – but to my mind this would be just as retrogressive a step as altering the offside law. Do we want football cheapened? Certainly not. If we stop to consider why people go to watch football, it's more than likely because of the fierce competitive element in our game.

I don't go along with those who say there are things drastically wrong with English football. Look around. We are still producing good players and excellent club sides in the hardest and most competitive league in the world. Even so, football is always seeking improvement, and it will undoubtedly be that our game of the future will angle itself more towards a European common denominator.

Football is highly progressive, and we are going to see a still more studious aproach. But I have yet to see anything in Europe to touch a really good English First Division match. We give better value for money in all-out commitment than in any other country, and a First Division game here is the ultimate in physical and mental application. English football's strong point is our total commitment. If we can retain this at the same time as learning a more thoughtful approach, we will get the best of both worlds.

I can see the day coming when more of our teams copy the Continental pattern of having a spare man at the back of the defence. When the Italians first introduced this, the man was called a stopper, but football has evolved so much in Europe that he is now a starter. Continental sides don't scheme and plot from midfield – they do it from defence, and the Italians' own sterile approach of a few years back has been superseded by a similar plan using far more imagination.

It would be interesting to look into the future right now to see if English football will get that way. I think it will, and that it will be popular with the fans. We can never expect a return to the mass attendances that we saw in the early post-war years, when the British working man had so little else to occupy his time. Football must accept this...not gripe about it.

Is there a future for the existing Football League of 92 clubs? I believe there is, providing clubs in the lower divisions are prepared to accept part-time players. This has been done on the Continent for years, with no resultant fall in the playing standard, so there is no reason why it should not work here. If clubs complain that they cannot pay their way, then why not go part-time? That, surely, is better than going out of business. The game would certainly not suffer, but it would still retain its corporate strength.

Our football, contrary to what many people may try to tell you, is improving all the time. Lower division sides are better organised than ever before; a lot of bright young men are coming in as managers and coaches; all this can only be for the good of the game. New ideas will improve others long tried and tested. Natural evolution will bring about even more improved football.

There will still be no guarantee of success, of course. Nor can there ever be. But it's my belief that success goes to the deserving and we must be prepared to work harder than ever so that Chelsea's future on the field matches the exciting progress that is being made around the ground.

WANTED: A CHELSEA GOALSCORER

As far as individual requirements on the field are concerned, one Chelsea need stands out above all others at the start of 1974-75. They must find a goalscorer. No, not a striker or a front-runner, to use the modern idiom, but a real, old-fashioned goalscorer. There **IS** a difference. If it is any comfort, twenty-one other clubs start the season hoping and praying that someone will knock in twenty or more First Division goals for them during the next nine months, but Chelsea's problem is greater than most and must be solved quickly if their two million pound stand is to be brought to life – noisy, cheering, throbbing, exciting life – on Saturday afternoons.

The near demise of goalscorers was inevitable as the tacticians switched the game's emphasis away from attack, changing the formation from 2-3-5 to 4-2-4 to 4-3-3 to 4-4-2. The malaise is world-wide. It's not what you score, but how little you concede, that wins prizes. Look at last season's League Championship: Leeds and Liverpool each gave away only 31 goals in 42 matches and finished first and second; Chelsea, seventeenth, scored 56 goals, and only two clubs did better – Champions Leeds with 66 goals and Ipswich (fourth) with 69.

As a further example of the way the game has changed to the detriment of goalscoring, the leading scorers in First Division football last season were Frank Worthington (Leicester City) and Mike Channon (Southampton) each with 20 goals – merely one third of the record 60 which Bill (Dixie) Dean scored for Everton in 1927-28.

The warning signs were flashing for Chelsea when the last five games of 1973-74 produced a solitary goal. For the first time in 23 seasons not one Chelsea player reached double-figures as a goalscorer. By early November Tommy Baldwin had netted nine in ten League appearances, and without adding to that total he was still top scorer when the season ended.

Tommy Lawton...Roy Bentley...Jimmy Greaves...Bobby Tambling...Barry Bridges...Peter Osgood. Internationals all,

WHAT WE WANT
MANNS
FOR SHOP

these have been the shooting stars of post-war Chelsea football. Another of comparable calibre and crowd appeal now has to be found, and if he is not already in the camp as an up-and-coming reserve who knows how to put a ball in the net (Steve Finnieston) or a youth team player of high potential (Teddy Maybank), then a lot of money has got to be spent to bring him to Stamford Bridge in the way that Lawton and Bentley were brought — via the transfer market.

Unless the game's tactics swing back from defence to attack, Jimmy Greaves's 41 First Division goals in season 1960-61 will remain forever a Chelsea record. In each of his four seasons of first-team football here (1957-61) he was the club's top scorer, with the phenomenal aggregate of 124 League goals in 157 appearances.

Greaves was a genius and goal-machine combined, a true striker years before the term was invented. With the goal that completed his hat-trick at home to Manchester City on November 19, 1960, Jimmy went in the record books as the first player to reach a century of League goals before the age of 21.

Hat-tricks, and better, were the Greaves hallmark, and on no fewer than 13 occasions he scored three or more goals in first-team football for Chelsea:-

Greaves may have performed the feat three times, but he was not Chelsea's first five-goals-in-a-match marksman. That distinction went half a century earlier to the club's original goalscoring sensation, George Hilsdon. This 19-year-old forward, signed from West Ham on a free transfer in the summer of 1906, made his debut at home to Glossop in the Second Division on September 1, the opening day of Chelsea's second season. The match was won 9-2 (still the club's biggest League victory) with Hilsdon scoring five times — a record that has never been equalled by a player making his League debut. The following season Chelsea beat Worksop 9-1 for their still-highest F.A. Cup score and Hilsdon bagged six of them. Not even Greaves could approach that all-time individual scoring record for Chelsea in F.A. Cup football.

JIMMY GREAVES, Chelsea's sharpest-ever marksman with 124 First Division goals in only four seasons. Part of his secret was superb balance, illustrated here in a match at Fulham

That left foot of BOBBY TAMBLING scored more than half his 202 first-team goals for Chelsea

CHELSEA & S
BUILDIN
SAVINGS

Bobby Tambling, the record aggregate scorer in Chelsea history with a grand total of 202 first-team goals, joined the club's exclusive 'five in a match' sharpshooters in the 6-2 League win away to Aston Villa in September 1966.

The fourth Chelsea man to net five times in a senior competitive match was Peter Osgood when Jeunesse Hautcharage, of Luxembourg, were defeated 13-0 in the European Cup-Winners' Cup first round second leg at Stamford Bridge in September 1971.

From large individual hauls we turn to great individual goals for Chelsea...and of all those by Jimmy Greaves the most spectacular, by general consent, was the first of his three at home to Birmingham in September 1959. With the game only three minutes old he collected the ball in his own half, swerved past five defenders in a dazzling 60-yard dribble and finished, as he nearly always did when the target was in his sights, with the perfect shot.

Did Peter Osgood ever score a more artistic goal at Stamford Bridge than when he loped through from his own half, beating four opponents on the way, against Southampton in September 1967? Rated even more remarkable by those who saw both goals was Osgood's solo run through the mud from deep midfield for the winner at Burnley in January 1966. 'Finest individual goal ever scored at Turf Moor,' declared many Burnley followers. Ossie's own recollection? 'We won 2-1 after being one down. I scored both, and the winner was from one of those long runs that look so good when they come off. It began just inside our half and I just kept going...and going...and going.'

As a 'big occasion' scorer Osgood will always be remembered at Chelsea for two particular Cup goals – his magnificently headed equaliser in the 1970 F.A. Cup Final replay against Leeds at Old Trafford and, a year later, his shot from the edge of the box that beat Real Madrid in Athens to bring the Cup Winners' Cup to Stamford Bridge.

An amazing goal by the unlikeliest of scorers proved Chelsea's League Cup winner in the 1965 Final against Leicester City. Because of injuries, Eddie McCreadie found himself switched from left-back to the role of makeshift

PETER OSGOOD, the star who gave a new word to the Chelsea vocabulary – the "Osgoal"

centre-forward on first-leg night, and early in the game Chelsea were reduced to ten men by injury to defender Allan Young. With ten minutes left, McCreadie set off on a run that carried him more than half the length of the muddy pitch and, after pushing the ball past Gordon Banks, he sat on his haunches on the edge of the penalty-area and watched it roll on into the net. That goal gave Chelsea a 3-2 victory, and with the second leg scoreless it brought the League Cup to Stamford Bridge.

Among other great individual Chelsea goals we recall is the John Hollins 'special' when Arsenal were beaten 2-1 at The Bridge in August 1970. This was Alan Hoby's description in the **Sunday Express:** 'Hollins scored the golden goal of the seventies for, whatever happens in the future, none of us, I am sure, will ever again see a goal quite like it. Rocketing through the middle like a blue streak, Hollins simultaneously killed Ron Harris's fine through pass and held off the hulking Roberts. Then, as 'keeper Bob Wilson came off his line, Hollins swerved breathtakingly to his left and, in full stride, chipped the ball over the horrified Wilson's head. Arsenal fans in the sweltering 53,722 crowd tensed in torment as a racketing roar rose from their Chelsea foes. But it was cut off abruptly as the ball rebounded from the bar. But Hollins, as if seized by a fever, sprinted on in a half-circle, outpaced the astounded Arsenal defence and, with his back to the goal, pounced on the ball again. Then, swivelling, he cracked it right foot into the back of the net. Wonderful.'

In a subsequent programme poll, supporters voted that the greatest individual goal seen at Stamford Bridge, and in the second place they put Alan Hudson's effort at home to Sheffield Wednesday in March 1970. Chelsea won 3-1 and Hudson, starting from just inside his own half, left four opponents trailing and finished with a shot to match his glorious run.

Ask Chelsea followers to name the most wonderful goal in the club's history and by a big majority the answer is David Webb's header that won the F.A. Cup five seasons ago. That goal turned lifelong dreams to reality, and without it there could have been no Cup-Winners' Cup success a year later.

Goals win matches — and cups. The fans join skipper Ron Harris, Tommy Baldwin and Charlie Cooke on a lap of honour in Athens after the defeat of Real Madrid in the 1971 Cup-Winners' Cup Final.

JOHN HOLLINS, Chelsea's penalty-taker, scores No. 4 from the spot on the night that Jeunesse goalkeeper picked 13 out of the net

May it be soon that goals of similar significance are scored again for Chelsea – a wish that leads back to the question with which this chapter started: Who will be the player to bring such goals to Stamford Bridge? For the stage, like the new £2,000,000 stand, is there, waiting to be filled by some new and exciting Chelsea hot-shot. Not a striker . . . nor a front-runner . . . but a fellow who can fulfil the most difficult role in modern football. Someone called a goalscorer.

Two views of one of the most spectacular goals ever scored at Stamford Bridge. Top: Eddie McCreadie, centre-forward for the night, toe-ends the ball past Gordon Banks at the end of an 80-yard run in the first leg of the 1965 League Cup Final against Leicester. Below: Arms raised in triumph, McCreadie sits back and watches his shot roll, roll, roll, for the goal, goal, goal that won the League Cup

The most wonderful Chelsea goal of all – DAVID WEBB's header that brought the F.A. Cup to Stamford Bridge in 1970

CFC

CHELSEA'S TOP SHOTS
IN THE 28 POST-WAR SEASONS

Season	Leading League Scorer	Goals	Appear ances	Goals Club Total	Final League Position
1946-47	Tommy Lawton	26	34	69	15th
1947-48	Ken Armstrong	11	42		18th
	Bobby Campbell	11	32	53	
1948-49	Roy Bentley	20	40	69	13th
1949-50	Roy Bentley	17	39		
	Hugh Billington	17	35	58	13th
1950-51	Roy Bentley	8	38	53	20th
1951-52	Roy Bentley	12	32		
	Jimmy D'Arcy	12	21	52	19th
1952-53	Roy Bentley	12	37	56	19th
1953-54	Roy Bentley	21	41	74	8th
1954-55	Roy Bentley	21	41	81	1st
1955-56	Roy Bentley	14	38	64	16th
1956-57	John McNichol	10	24		
	Ron Tindall	10	26	73	13th
1957-58	Jimmy Greaves	22	35	83	11th
1958-59	Jimmy Greaves	32	42	77	14th
1959-60	Jimmy Greaves	29	40	76	18th
1960-61	Jimmy Greaves	41	40	98	12th
1961-62	Bobby Tambling	20	34	63	22nd
*1962-63	Bobby Tambling	35	40	81	2nd
1963-64	Bobby Tambling	17	35	72	5th
1964-65	Barry Bridges	20	41	89	3rd
1965-66	George Graham	17	33	65	5th
1966-67	Bobby Tambling	21	36	67	9th
1967-68	Peter Osgood	16	42	62	6th
1968-69	Bobby Tambling	17	38	73	5th
1969-70	Peter Osgood	23	38	70	3rd
1070-71	Keith Weller	13	36	52	6th
1971-72	Peter Osgood	18	36	58	7th
1972-73	Chris Garland	11	27		
	Peter Osgood	11	38	49	12th
1973-74	Tommy Baldwin	9	19	56	17th

(*In Second Division)

Could STEVE FINNIESTON, 19-year-old Scotland Youth cap, be the answer to Chelsea's scoring problems this season? He showed he knew where the target is with 22 goals in 32 games as top reserve scorer last winter, and earned a place on the club's end-of-season tour of Australia

CHELSEA RECORDS

Chelsea's Complete Cup History

1905-1939: Every Chelsea F.A. Cup result, season by season (* = Extra time played. R = Replay)

SEASON 1905–06

(1st Qual. Rd.) 1st Grenadiers	(H)	W	6–1
(2nd Qual. Rd.) Southern United	(A)	W	1–0
(3rd Qual. Rd.) Crystal P.	(A)	L	1–7

SEASON 1906–07

(1) Lincoln C.	(A)	D	2–2
(R) Lincoln C.	(H)	L	0–1

SEASON 1907–08

(1) Worksop	(H)	W	9–1
(2) Manchester Utd.	(A)	L	0–1

SEASON 1908–09

(1) Hull C.	(A)	D	1–1
(R) Hull C.	(H)	W	1–0
(2) Blackburn R.	(A)	L	1–2

SEASON 1909–10

(1) Hull C.	(H)	W	2–1
(2) Tottenham H.	(H)	L	0–1

SEASON 1910–11

(1) Leyton	(H)	D	0–0
(R) Leyton	(A)	W	2–0
(2) Chesterfield	(A)	W	4–1
(3) Wolverhampton W.	(A)	W	2–0
(4) Swindon T.	(H)	W	3–1
(S.f.) Newcastle U.	(Birmingham)	L	0–3

SEASON 1911–12

(1) Sheffield U.	(H)	W	1–0
(2) Bradford C.	(A)	L	0–2

SEASON 1912–13

(1) Southend U.	(H)	W	5–2
(2) Sheffield W.	(H)	D	1–1
(R) Sheffield W.	(A)	L	0–6

SEASON 1913–14

(1) Millwall	(A)	D	0–0
(R) Millwall	(H)	L	0–1

SEASON 1914–15

(1) Swindon T.	(H)	D	1–1
(R) Swindon T. (by arrangement)	(H)	W	5–2
(2) Arsenal	(H)	W	1–0
(3) Manchester C.	(A)	W	1–0
(4) Newcastle U.	(H)	D	1–1*
(R) Newcastle U.	(A)	W	1–0
(S.f.) Everton	(Villa Park)	W	2–0
(F) Sheffield U.	(Old Trafford)	L	0–3

SEASON 1919–20

(1) Bolton W.	(A)	W	1–0
(2) Swindon T.	(H)	W	4–0
(3) Leicester C.	(H)	W	3–0
(4) Bradford	(H)	W	4–1
(S.f.) Aston V.	(Bramall Lane, Sheffield)	L	1–3

SEASON 1920–21

(1) Reading	(A)	D	0–0
(R) Reading	(H)	D	2–2*
(R) Reading	(H)	W	3–1
(2) Swindon T.	(A)	W	2–0
(3) Plymouth A.	(A)	D	0–0
(R) Plymouth A	(H)	D	0–0*
(R) Plymouth A.	(Ashton Gate, Bristol)	W	2–1
(4) Cardiff C.	(A)	L	0–1

SEASON 1921–22

(1) W.B.A.	(H)	L	2–4

SEASON 1922–23

(1) Rotherham Co.	(H)	W	1–0
(2) Southampton	(H)	D	0–0
(R) Southampton	(A)	L	0–1

SEASON 1923–24

(1) Southampton	(H)	D	1–1
(R) Southampton	(A)	L	0–2

SEASON 1924–25

(1) Birmingham	(A)	L	0–2

SEASON 1925–26

(3) Plymouth A.	(A)	W	2–1
(4) Crystal P.	(A)	L	1–2

SEASON 1926–27

(3) Luton T.	(H)	W	4–0
(4) Accrington St.	(H)	W	7–2
(5) Burnley	(H)	W	2–1
(6) Cardiff C.	(H)	D	0–0
(R) Cardiff C.	(A)	L	2–3

SEASON 1927–28

(3) Wolverhampton W.	(A)	L	1–2

SEASON 1928–29

(3) Everton	(H)	W	2–0
(4) Birmingham	(H)	W	1–0
(5) Portsmouth	(H)	D	1–1
(R) Portsmouth	(A)	L	0–1

SEASON 1929–30

(3) Arsenal	(A)	L	0–2

SEASON 1930–31

(3) West Ham U.	(A)	W	3–1
(4) Arsenal	(H)	W	2–1
(5) Blackburn R.	(H)	W	3–0
(6) Birmingham	(A)	D	2–2
(R) Birmingham	(H)	L	0–3

SEASON 1931–32

(3) Tranmere R.	(A)	D	2–2
(R) Tranmere R.	(H)	W	5–3
(4) West Ham U.	(H)	W	3–1
(5) Sheffield W.	(A)	D	1–1
(R) Sheffield W.	(H)	W	2–0
(6) Liverpool	(A)	W	2–0
(S.f.) Newcastle U.	(Huddersfield)	L	1–2

SEASON 1932–33

(3) Brighton & H. A.	(A)	L	1–2

SEASON 1933–34

(3) W.B.A.	(H)	D	1–1
(R) W.B.A.	(A)	W	1–0
(4) Nottingham F.	(H)	D	1–1
(R) Nottingham F.	(A)	W	3–0
(5) Stoke C.	(A)	L	1–3

SEASON 1934–35

(3) Luton T.	(H)	D	1–1
(R) Luton T.	(A)	L	0–2

SEASON 1935–36

(3) Norwich C.	(A)	D	1–1
(R) Norwich C.	(H)	W	3–1
(4) Plymouth A.	(H)	W	4–1
(5) Fulham	(H)	D	0–0
(R) Fulham	(A)	L	2–3

SEASON 1936–37

(3) Leeds U.	(H)	W	4–0
(4) Millwall	(A)	L	0–3

SEASON 1937–38

(3) Everton	(H)	L	0–1

SEASON 1938–39

(3) Arsenal	(H)	W	2–1
(4) Fulham	(H)	W	3–0
(5) Sheffield W.	(H)	D	1–1
(R) Sheffield W.	(A)	D	0–0*
(R) Sheffield W.	(Highbury)	W	3–1
(6) Grimsby T.	(H)	L	0–1

1945 to date: Every Chelsea result, with appearances and goalscorers, season by season in F.A. Cup, Football League Cup, Fairs Cup and European Cup-Winners' Cup.

(* = Extra time played. R = Replay. Figures in brackets against players' names since 1966 = appearances as substitute).

SEASON 1945–46
[F.A. CUP]

(Competition played on Home and Away basis)

(3)	Leicester C.	(H)	D	1–1
	Leicester C.	(A)	W	2–0
	(Won 3–1 on aggregate)			
(4)	West Ham U.	(H)	W	2–0
	West Ham U.	(A)	L	0–1
	(Won 2–1 on aggregate)			
(5)	Aston V.	(H)	L	0–1
	Aston V.	(A)	L	0–1
	(Lost 0–2 on aggregate)			

J. Harris	6	J. Bain	5
T. Lawton	6	S. R. Foss	5
W. H. Robertson	6	J. Payne	5
R. Spence	6	L. Goulden	3
A. Tennant	6	A. Machin	3
R. Williams	6	R. Russell	2
D. Winter	6	D. L. Dolding	1

Goalscorers: Goulden 1, Lawton 1, Machin 1, Spence 1, Williams 1. **Total** 5.

SEASON 1946–47
[F.A. CUP]

(3)	Arsenal	(H)	D	1–1
(R)	Arsenal	(A)	D	1–1*
(R)	Arsenal (Tottenham)		W	2–0
(4)	Derby Co.	(H)	D	2–2
(R)	Derby Co.	(A)	L	0–1*

L. Goulden	5	T. Walker	5
T. Lawton	5	J. Harris	4
J. Macaulay	5	R. Spence	4
A. Machin	5	D. Winter	4
H. Medhurst	5	S. Bathgate	1
J. Paton	5	A. White	1
W. Steffen	5	R. Williams	1

Goalscorers: Lawton 4, Walker 1, Williams 1. **Total** 6.

SEASON 1947–48
[F.A. CUP]

(3)	Barrow	(H)	W	5–0
(4)	Manchester C.	(A)	L	0–2*

K. Armstrong	2	T. Walker	2
S. Bathgate	2	D. Winter	2
R. Campbell	2	R. Bentley	1
S. R. Foss	2	J. Bowie	1
L. Goulden	2	R. Goddard	1
T. B. Jones	2	J. Harris	1
H. Medhurst	2		

Goalscorers: Armstrong 2, Bowie 1, Campbell 1, Goulden 1. **Total** 5.

SEASON 1948–49
[F.A. CUP]

(3)	Bristol C.	(A) W	3–1
(4)	Everton	(H) W	2–0
(5)	W.B.A.	(A) L	0–3

K. Armstrong	3	F. Lewis	3
R. Bentley	3	J. Macaulay	3
J. Bowie	3	R. Williams	3
R. Campbell	3	D. Winter	3
J. Harris	3	P. Pickering	2
T. B. Jones	3	H. Medhurst	1

Goalscorers: Bentley 2, Bowie 1, Jones 1, Williams 1. **Total** 5.

SEASON 1949–50
[F.A. CUP]

(3)	Brentford	(A) W	1–0
(4)	Newcastle U.	(H) W	3–0
(5)	Chesterfield	(A) D	1–1
(R)	Chesterfield	(H) W	3–0
(6)	Manchester U.	(H) W	2–0
(S-f)	Arsenal (Tottenham)	D	2–2
(R)	Arsenal (Tottenham)	L	0–1*

K. Armstrong	7	H. Billington	6
W. Gray	7	R. Campbell	6
W. Hughes	7	J. Harris	6
H. Medhurst	7	J. Bowie	4
F. Mitchell	7	R. Williams	4
D. Winter	7	L. Goulden	2
R. Bentley	6	F. J. Saunders	1

Goalscorers: Bentley 5, Billington 3, Bowie 2, Campbell 2. **Total** 12.

SEASON 1950–51
[F.A. CUP]

(3)	Rochdale	(A) W	3–2
(4)	Exeter C.	(A) D	1–1
(R)	Exeter C.	(H) W	2–0
(5)	Fulham	(H) D	1–1
(R)	Fulham	(A) L	0–3

K. Armstrong	5	W. Dickson	4
R. Bentley	5	S. Bathgate	3
W. Gray	5	W. Hinshelwood	2
J. Harris	5	R. Williams	2
W. Hughes	5	D. Winter	2
P. Pickering	5	H. Billington	1
R. Smith	5	C. Dyke	1
R. Campbell	4	F. Mitchell	1

Goalscorers: Bentley 3, Smith 2, Billington 1, Williams 1. **Total** 7.

SEASON 1951–52
[F.A. CUP]

(3)	Chester	(H) D	2–2
(R)	Chester	(A) W	3–2*
(4)	Tranmere R.	(H) W	4–0
(5)	Leeds U.	(A) D	1–1
(R)	Leeds U.	(H) D	1–1*
(R)	Leeds U. (Villa Park)	W	5–1
(6)	Sheffield U.	(A) W	1–0
(S-f)	Arsenal (Tottenham)	D	1–1
(R)	Arsenal (Tottenham)	L	0–3

K. Armstrong	9	R. Smith	7
R. Bentley	9	S. Bathgate	6
W. Gray	9	R. Campbell	4
J. Harris	9	J. Smith	4
W. G. Robertson	9	S. Willemse	4
S. D'Arcy	8	T. B. Jones	2
S. Tickridge	8	F. Mitchell	2
W. Dickson	7	E. Parsons	2

Goalscorers: Bentley 5, R. Smith 5, Gray 3, Armstrong 2, D'Arcy 1, Jones 1, Opponent 1. **Total** 18.

SEASON 1952–53
[F.A. CUP]

(3)	Derby Co.	(A)	D	4–4
(R)	Derby Co.	(H)	W	1–0*
(4)	W.B.A.	(H)	D	1–1
(R)	W.B.A.	(A)	D	0–0*
(R)	W.B.A. (Villa Park)		D	1–1*
(R)	W.B.A. (Highbury)		W	4–0
(5)	Birmingham	(H)	L	0–4

K. Armstrong	7	S. Willemse	7
R. Bentley	7	R. Campbell	6
W. Dickson	7	W. Gray	5
J. McNichol	7	S. Tickridge	4
E. Parsons	7	J. Harris	3
F. J. Saunders	7	M. Spector	3
C. Thomson	7		

Goalscorers: Bentley 5, Parsons 3, Armstrong 1, Campbell 1, McNichol 1. **Total** 11.

SEASON 1953–54
[F.A. CUP]

(3)	W.B.A.	(A)	L	0–1

K. Armstrong	1	E. Parsons	1
R. Bentley	1	D. Saunders	1
F. Blunstone	1	L. Stubbs	1
R. Greenwood	1	C. Thomson	1
J. Harris	1	S. Willemse	1
J. McNichol	1		

SEASON 1954–55
[F.A. CUP]

(3)	Walsall	(H)	W	2–0
(4)	Bristol R.	(A)	W	3–1
(5)	Notts Co.	(A)	L	0–1

K. Armstrong	3	S. Wicks	3
R. Bentley	3	S. Willemse	3
F. Blunstone	3	J. McNichol	2
E. Parsons	3	C. Thomson	2
D. Saunders	3	S. O'Connell	1
P. Sillett	3	W. G. Robertson	1
L. Stubbs	3		

Goalscorers: Blunstone 1, McNichol 1, O'Connell 1, Parsons 1, Stubbs 1. **Total** 5.

SEASON 1955–56
[F.A. CUP]

(3)	Hartlepools U.	(A)	W	1–0
(4)	Burnley	(A)	D	1–1
(R)	Burnley	(H)	D	1–1*
(R)	Burnley (Birmingham)		D	2–2*
(R)	Burnley (Arsenal)		D	0–0*
(R)	Burnley (Tottenham)		W	2–0
(5)	Everton	(A)	L	0–1

R. Bentley	7	W. G. Robertson	4
F. Blunstone	7	L. Stubbs	4
D. Saunders	7	B. Nicholas	3
P. Sillett	7	C. Thomson	3
S. Willemse	7	R. Tindall	3
J. McNichol	6	J Lewis	2
S. Wicks	6	P. Brabrook	1
E. Parsons	5	W. Livingstone	1
A. Dicks	4		

Goalscorers: Bentley 1, Blunstone 1, Lewis 1, Parsons 1, Sillett 1, Tindall 1, Opponent 1. **Total** 7.

SEASON 1956–57
[F.A. CUP]

(3)	Leyton O.	(A)	W	2–0
(4)	Tottenham H.	(A)	L	0–4

K. Armstrong	2	A. Dicks	1
F. Blunstone	2	W. Livingstone	1
P. Brabrook	2	A. Nicholas	1
R. Matthews	2	J. Sillett	1
J. McNichol	2	L. Stubbs	1
D. Saunders	2	R. Tindall	1
P. Sillett	2	R. Whittaker	1
L. Allen	1		

Goalscorers: Brabrook 1, McNichol 1. **Total** 2.

SEASON 1957–58
[F.A. CUP]

(3)	Doncaster R.	(A)	W	2–0
(4)	Darlington	(H)	D	3–3
(R)	Darlington	(A)	L	1–4*

P. Brabrook	3	P. Sillett	3
L. Casey	3	D. Saunders	3
J. Lewis	3	J. Greaves	2
I. MacFarlane	3	R. Tindall	2
R. Matthews	3	L. Allen	1
J. McNichol	3	L. Stubbs	1
J. Mortimore	3		

Goalscorers: McNichol 4, Lewis 1, Tindall 1. **Total** 6.

SEASON 1958–59
[F.A. CUP]

(3)	Newcastle U.	(A)	W	4–1
(4)	Aston V.	(H)	L	1–2

M. Block	2	M. Scott	2
P. Brabrook	2	J. Sillett	2
S. Crowther	2	P. Sillett	2
D. Gibbs	2	R. Tindall	2
J. Greaves	2	J. Mortimore	1
R. Matthews	2	D. Saunders	1

Goalscorers: Greaves 2, Brabrook 1, Gibbs 1, Mortimore 1. **Total** 5.

[FAIRS CUP]

(1) Frem, Copenhagen (Denmark) (A) W 3–1
Frem, Copenhagen (H) W 4–1
(Won 7–2 on aggregate)

(2) Red Star, Belgrade (H) W 1–0
Red Star, Belgrade (A) L 1–4
(Lost 2–4 on aggregate)

P. Sillett	4	A. Nicholas	2
L. Allen	3	D. Saunders	2
P. Brabrook	3	M. Scott	2
J. Greaves	3	J. Sillett	2
M. Harrison	3	R. Tindall	2
R. Matthews	3	R. Whittaker	2
J. Mortimore	3	M. Block	1
S. Anderton	2	D. Court	1
F. Blunstone	2	C. Huxford	1
S. Crowther	2	W. G. Robertson	1

Goalscorers: Greaves 3, Brabrook 2, Harrison 1, Nicholas 1, P. Sillett 1, Opponent 1. **Total** 9.

SEASON 1959–60

[F.A. CUP]

(3) Bradford (H) W 5–1
(4) Aston V. (H) L 1–2

S. Anderton	2	C. Livesey	2
F. Blunstone	2	R. Matthews	2
P. Brabrook	2	M. Scott	2
J. Brooks	2	J. Sillett	2
S. Crowther	2	P. Sillett	2
J. Greaves	2		

Goalscorers: Brabrook 2, Blunstone 1, Greaves 1, Livesey 1, P. Sillett 1. **Total** 6.

SEASON 1960–61

[F.A. CUP]

(3) Crewe Alexandra (H) L 1–2

S. Anderton	1	A. Harris	1
F. Blunstone	1	P. Sillett	1
P. Bonetti	1	R. Tambling	1
P. Brabrook	1	R. Tindall	1
R. Evans	1	T. Venables	1
J. Greaves	1		

Goalscorer: Blunstone 1. **Total** 1.

[FOOTBALL LEAGUE CUP]

(1) Millwall (A) W 7–1
(2) Workington (H) W 4–2
(3) Doncaster R. (A) W 7–0
(4) Portsmouth (A) L 0–1

P. Brabrook	4	T. Venables	3
J. Brooks	4	F. Blunstone	2
R. Evans	4	J. Greaves	2
P. Bonetti	3	J. Sillett	2
A. Harris	3	S. Anderton	1
J. Mortimore	3	S. Crowther	1
P. Sillett	3	C. Livesey	1
R. Tambling	3	R. Matthews	1
R. Tindall	3	A. Nicholas	1

Goalscorers: Brabrook 4, Tambling 3, Blunstone 2, Greaves 2, P. Sillett 2, Brooks 1, Evans 1, Mortimore 1, Nicholas 1, J. Sillett 1. **Total** 18.

SEASON 1961–62
[F.A. CUP]

(3) Liverpool (A) L 3–4

F. Blunstone	1	A. Murray	1
P. Bonetti	1	M. Scott	1
P. Brabrook	1	K. Shellito	1
B. Bridges	1	R. Tambling	1
A. Harris	1	A. Young	1
A. Malcolm	1		

Goalscorers: Tambling 2, Bridges 1. **Total** 3.

SEASON 1962–63
[F.A. CUP]

(3) Tranmere R. (A) D 2–2
(R) Tranmere R. (H) W 3–1
(4) Charlton A. (A) W 3–0
(5) Manchester U. (A) L 1–2

F. Blunstone	4	K. Shellito	3
P. Bonetti	4	B. Bridges	2
G. Moore	4	A. Harris	2
J. Mortimore	4	E. McCreadie	2
A. Murray	4	J. Mulholland	1
R. Tambling	4	D. Sorrell	1
F. Upton	4	I. Watson	1
T. Venables	4		

Goalscorers: Bridges 2, Tambling 2, Moore 1, Mulholland 1, Murr 1, Sorrell 1, Venables 1. **Total** 9.

SEASON 1963–64
[F.A. CUP]

(3) Tottenham H. (A) D 1–1
(R) Tottenham H. (H) W 2–0
(4) Huddersfield T. (H) L 1–2

F. Blunstone	3	J. Mortimore	3
B. Bridges	3	A. Murray	3
J. Dunn	3	F. Upton	3
R. Harris	3	T. Venables	3
M. Hinton	3	R. Tambling	2
E. McCreadie	3	D. Brown	1

Goalscorers: Murray 2, Tambling 2. **Total** 4.

[FOOTBALL LEAGUE CUP]

(2) Swindon T. (A) L 0–3

F. Blunstone	1	M. Hinton	1
P. Bonetti	1	J. Hollins	1
D. Brown	1	E. McCreadie	1
T. Harmer	1	J. O'Rourke	1
A. Harris	1	R. Tambling	1
R. Harris	1		

SEASON 1964–65
[F.A. CUP]

(3) Northampton T. (H) W 4–1
(4) West Ham U. (A) W 1–0
(5) Tottenham H. (H) W 1–0
(6) Peterborough T. (H) W 5–1
(S-f) Liverpool (Villa Park) L 0–2

P. Bonetti	5	A. Murray	5
B. Bridges	5	R. Tambling	5
G. Graham	5	T. Venables	5
R. Harris	5	J. Boyle	2
M. Hinton	5	E. McCreadie	2
J. Hollins	5	F. Upton	1
J. Mortimore	5		

Goalscorers: Bridges 4, Tambling 4, Hollins 1, Murray 1, Opponent 1. **Total** 11.

[FOOTBALL LEAGUE CUP (Winners)]

(2)	Birmingham C.	(A) W	3–0
(3)	Notts Co.	(H) W	4–0
(4)	Swansea T.	(H) W	3–2
(5)	Workington	(A) D	2–2
(R)	Workington	(H) W	2–0
(S-f 1)	Aston V.	(A) W	3–2
(S-f 2)	Aston V.	(H) D	1–1
	(Won 4–3 on aggregate)		
(F 1)	Leicester C.	(H) W	3–2
(F 2)	Leicester C.	(A) D	0–0
	(Won 3–2 on aggregate)		

P. Bonetti	9	J. Boyle	4
J. Mortimore	8	F. Upton	4
G. Graham	7	J. Fascione	3
R. Tambling	7	P. Houseman	3
R. Harris	6	I. Watson	3
M. Hinton	6	A. Harris	2
J. Hollins	6	D. Brown	1
A. Murray	6	T. Knox	1
B. Bridges	5	P. Osgood	1
J. McCalliog	5	K. Shellito	1
E. McCreadie	5	A. Young	1
T. Venables	5		

Goalscorers: Tambling 6, Graham 4, Bridges 3, Osgood 2, Boyle 1, Brown 1, A. Harris 1, McCalliog 1, McCreadie 1, Venables 1. **Total** 21.

SEASON 1965–66

[F.A. CUP]

(3)	Liverpool	(A) W	2–1
(4)	Leeds U.	(H) W	1–0
(5)	Shrewsbury T.	(H) W	3–2
(6)	Hull C.	(H) D	2–2
(R)	Hull C.	(A) W	3–1
(S-f)	Sheffield W. (Villa Pk.)	L	0–2

P. Bonetti	6	J. Boyle	5
B. Bridges	6	J. Hollins	5
G. Graham	6	E. McCreadie	5
R. Harris	6	P. Osgood	5
M. Hinton	6	J. Kirkup	3
R. Tambling	6	A. Murray	1
T. Venables	6		

Goalscorers: Tambling 5, Graham 3, Bridges 2, Osgood 1. **Total** 11.

[FAIRS CUP]

(1)	A.S. Roma (Italy)	(H)	W	4–1
	A.S. Roma	(A)	D	0–0
	(Won 4–1 on aggregate)			
(2)	Wiener S.C. (Austria)	(A)	L	0–1
	Wiener S.C.	(H)	W	2–0
	(Won 2–1 on aggregate)			
(3)	A.C. Milan (Italy)	(A)	L	1–2
	A.C. Milan	(H)	W	2–1
Play off	A.C. Milan	(A)	D	1–1*
	(Agg. result: 4–4. Chelsea won tie on toss)			
(4)	T.S.V. Munich 1860 (W. Germany)	(A)	D	2–2
	T.S.V. Munich	(H)	W	1–0
	(Won 3–2 on aggregate)			
(S-f)	C.F. Barcelona (Spain)	(A)	L	0–2
	C.F. Barcelona	(H)	W	2–0
Play-off	C.F. Barcelona	(A)	L	0–5
	(Lost 2–7 on aggregate)			

P. Bonetti	12	B. Bridges	7
J. Hollins	12	J. Kirkup	5
G. Graham	11	K. Shellito	4
M. Hinton	11	A. Murray	3
P. Osgood	11	A. Young	3
R. Harris	10	C. Cooke	2
R. Tambling	10	J. Fascione	2
E. McCreadie	9	A. Harris	2
J. Boyle	8	P. Houseman	2
T. Venables	8		

Goalscorers: Graham 3, Osgood 3, Venables 3, Tambling 2, Bridges 1, Murray 1, Opponents 2. **Total** 15.

SEASON 1966–67

[F.A. CUP]

(3)	Huddersfield T.	(A)	W	2–1
(4)	Brighton & H.A.	(A)	D	1–1
(R)	Brighton & H.A.	(H)	W	4–0
(5)	Sheffield U.	(H)	W	2–0
(6)	Sheffield W.	(H)	W	1–0
(S-f)	Leeds U. (Villa Park)		W	1–0
(F)	Tottenham H. (Wembley)		L	1–2

T. Baldwin	7	C. Cooke	6 (1)
P. Bonetti	7	A. Hateley	6
R. Harris	7	A. Harris	3 (1)
M. Hinton	7	J. Thomson	3
J. Hollins	7	J. Kirkup	2 (1)
E. McCreadie	7	P. Houseman	1
R. Tambling	7	A. Young	1
J. Boyle	6		

Goalscorers: Tambling 6, Hateley 3, Baldwin 1, Houseman 1, Young 1. **Total** 12.

[FOOTBALL LEAGUE CUP]

(2)	Charlton A.	(H)	W	5–2
(3)	Blackpool	(A)	D	1–1
(R)	Blackpool	(H)	L	1–3

P. Bonetti	3	R. Tambling	3
J. Boyle	3	P. Houseman	2 (1)
C. Cooke	3	E. McCreadie	2
R. Harris	3	P. Osgood	2
M. Hinton	3	G. Graham	1
J. Hollins	3	A. Harris	1 (1)
J. Kirkup	3	J. Thomson	1

Goalscorers: Houseman 3, Graham 1, Hollins 1, Tambling 1, Opponent 1. **Total** 7.

SEASON 1967–68

[F.A. CUP]

(3)	Ipswich T.	(H) W	3–0
(4)	Norwich C.	(H) W	1–0
(5)	Sheffield W.	(A) D	2–2
(R)	Sheffield W.	(H) W	2–0
(6)	Birmingham C.	(A) L	0–1

A. Birchenall	5	R. Tambling	5	
P. Bonetti	5	T. Baldwin	4	
C. Cooke	5	J. Boyle	4	
R. Harris	5	M. Hinton	2	
J. Hollins	5	P. Houseman	2	
E. McCreadie	5	J. Thomson	2	(1)
P. Osgood	5	J. Kirkup	1	(1)

Goalscorers: Tambling 3, Birchenall 2, Baldwin 1, Cooke 1, Osgood 1 **Total** 8.

[FOOTBALL LEAGUE CUP]

(2)	Middlesbrough	(A) L	1–2

T. Baldwin	1	E. McCreadie	1	
P. Bonetti	1	P. Osgood	1	
C. Cooke	1	R. Tambling	1	
R. Harris	1	J. Thomson	1	
J. Hollins	1	C. Waldron	1	
P. Houseman	1	M. Hinton	–	(1)

Goalscorer: Cooke 1. **Total** 1.

SEASON 1968–69

[F.A. CUP]

(3)	Carlisle U.	(H) W	2–0
(4)	Preston N.E.	(A) D	0–0
(R)	Preston N.E. (Abandoned 75 minutes—floodlight failure)	(H)	2–0
(R)	Preston N.E.	(H) W	2–1
(5)	Stoke C.	(H) W	3–2
(6)	W.B.A.	(H) L	1–2

A. Birchenall	5	R. Tambling	5	
P. Bonetti	5	D. Webb	5	
C. Cooke	5	J. Boyle	4	(1)
R. Harris	5	S. Houston	3	
J. Hollins	5	P. Houseman	2	
E. McCreadie	5	J. Dempsey	1	
P. Osgood	5			

Goalscorers: Osgood 3, Webb 2, Birchenall 1, Cooke 1, Tambling 1. **Total** 8.

[FOOTBALL LEAGUE CUP]

(2)	Birmingham C.	(A) W	1–0
(3)	Derby Co.	(H) D	0–0
(R)	Derby Co.	(A) L	1–3

A. Birchenall	3	D. Webb	3	
P. Bonetti	3	T. Baldwin	2	
R. Harris	3	J. Boyle	2	
J. Hollins	3	C. Cooke	2	
E. McCreadie	3	M. Hinton	1	(1)
P. Osgood	3	P. Houseman	1	
R. Tambling	3	I. Hutchinson	1	

Goalscorers: Birchenall 1, Opponent 1. **Total** 2.

[FAIRS CUP]

(1) Morton (Scotland) (H) W 5–0
Morton (A) W 4–3
(Won 9–3 on aggregate)
(2) D.W.S. Amsterdam (Holland) (H) D 0–0
D.W.S. Amsterdam (A) D 0–0*
(Aggregate result: 0–0 Chelsea lost tie on toss)

T. Baldwin	4	J. Boyle	3	
A. Birchenall	4	C. Cooke	3	
P. Bonetti	4	J. Hollins	3	
R. Harris	4	P. Osgood	3	(1)
E. McCreadie	4	M. Hinton	2	
R. Tambling	4	P. Houseman	2	
D. Webb	4			

Goalscorers: Birchenall 2, Baldwin 1, Boyle 1, Cooke 1, Hollins 1, Houseman 1, Osgood 1, Tambling 1. **Total** 9.

SEASON 1969–70

[F.A. CUP (Winners)]

(3) Birmingham C. (H) W 3–0
(4) Burnley (H) D 2–2
(R) Burnley (A) W 3–1*
(R) Crystal P. (A) W 4–1
(6) Q.P.R. (A) W 4–2
(S-f) Watford (Tottenham) W 5–1
(F) Leeds. U. (Wembley) D 2–2*
(R) Leeds U. (Old Trafford) W 2–1*

P. Bonetti	8	D. Webb	8	
J. Dempsey	8	P. Osgood	7	
R. Harris	8	C. Cooke	6	
J. Hollins	8	A. Hudson	6	
P. Houseman	8	T. Baldwin	5	
I. Hutchinson	8	M. Hinton	–	(2)
E. McCreadie	8			

Goalscorers: Osgood 8, Houseman 6, Hutchinson 5, Webb 3, Baldwin 1, Dempsey 1, Hollins 1. **Total** 25.

[FOOTBALL LEAGUE CUP]

(2) Coventry C. (A) W 1–0
(3) Leeds U. (A) D 1–1
(R) Leeds U. (H) W 2–0
(4) Carlisle U. (A) L 0–1

A. Birchenall	4	P. Osgood	3	
P. Bonetti	4	D. Webb	3	
M. Hinton	4	C. Cooke	2	(1)
J. Hollins	4	A. Hudson	2	
P. Houseman	4	E. McCreadie	2	
J. Boyle	3	T. Baldwin	1	
J. Dempsey	3	S. Houston	1	
R. Harris	3	I. Hutchinson	1	

Goalscorers: Birchenall 2, Cooke 1, Hutchinson 1. **Total** 4.

SEASON 1970–71

[F.A. CUP]

(3) Crystal P. (A) D 2–2
(R) Crystal P. (H) W 2–0
(4) Manchester C. (H) L 0–3

P. Bonetti	3	P. Osgood	3
J. Boyle	3	D. Webb	3
C. Cooke	3	K. Weller	3
R. Harris	3	T. Baldwin	2
M. Hinton	3	I. Hutchinson	1
J. Hollins	3	J. Dempsey	– (1)
P. Houseman	3		

Goalscorers: Baldwin 2, Houseman 1, Osgood 1. **Total** 4.

[FOOTBALL LEAGUE CUP]

(2) Sheffield W.	(A) D 1–1	(3) Middlesbrough	(H) W 3–2
(R) Sheffield W.	(H) W 2–1	(4) Manchester U.	(A) L 1–2

P. Bonetti	4	K. Weller	3
R. Harris	4	T. Baldwin	2
J. Hollins	4	J. Dempsey	2
P. Houseman	4	M. Hinton	2
D. Webb	4	J. Boyle	1
C. Cooke	3	A. Hudson	1
I. Hutchinson	3	D. Smethurst	1
P. Mulligan	3	S. Houston	– (1)
P. Osgood	3		

Goalscorers: Osgood 2, Baldwin 1, Hollins 1, Hutchinson 1, Webb 1, Weller 1. **Total** 7.

[EUROPEAN CUP-WINNERS' CUP (WINNERS)]

(1) Aris (Greece) (A) D 1–1
(1) Aris (H) W 5–1
(Won 6–2 on aggregate)
(2) C.S.K.A. Sofia (Bulgaria) (A) W 1–0
(2) C.S.K.A. Sofia (H) W 1–0
(Won 2–0 on aggregate)
(Q-f 1) Bruges (Belgium) (A) L 0–2
(Q-f 2) Bruges (H) W 4–0*
(Won 4–2 on aggregate)
(S-f 1) Manchester C. (H) W 1–0
(S-f 2) Manchester C. (A) W 1–0
(Won 2–0 on aggregate)
(F 1) Real Madrid (Spain) (Athens) D 1–1*
(R) Real Madrid (Athens) W 2–1

D. Webb	10	P. Mulligan	5 (1)
R. Harris	9	J. Boyle	5 (2)
A. Hudson	9	J. Phillips	4
J. Hollins	8	T. Baldwin	4 (3)
K. Weller	8 (1)	M. Hinton	3
C. Cooke	8	I. Hutchinson	3
P. Houseman	8	D. Smethurst	3 (1)
J. Dempsey	7	E. McCreadie	2
P. Osgood	7	M. Droy	1
P. Bonetti	6		

Goalscorers: Osgood 4, Hutchinson 3, Baldwin 2, Hollins 2, Dempsey 1, Hinton 1, Houseman 1, Smethurst 1, Webb 1, Opponent 1. **Total** 17.

SEASON 1971–72

[F.A. CUP]

(3) Blackpool (A) W 1–0
(4) Bolton W. (H) W 3–0
(5) Orient (A) L 2–3

P. Bonetti	3	P. Osgood	3
C. Cooke	3	D. Webb	3
R. Harris	3	S. Kember	2 (1)
J. Hollins	3	J. Dempsey	2
P. Houseman	3	C. Garland	1
A. Hudson	3	E. McCreadie	1
P. Mulligan	3		

Goalscorers: Cooke 1, Dempsey 1, Hollins 1, Houseman 1, Osgood 1 Webb 1. **Total** 6.

[FOOTBALL LEAGUE CUP]

(2)	Plymouth A.	(H) W	2–0
(3)	Nottingham F.	(A) D	1–1
(R)	Nottingham F.	(H) W	2–1
(4)	Bolton W.	(H) D	1–1
(R)	Bolton W.	(A) W	6–0.
(5)	Norwich C.	(A) W	1–0
(S-f 1)	Tottenham H.	(H) W	3–2
(S-f 2)	Tottenham H.	(A) D	2–2
	(Won 5–4 on aggregate)		
(F)	Stoke C. (Wembley)	L	1–2

R. Harris	9	J. Boyle	6	
J. Hollins	9	T. Baldwin	5	(2)
A. Hudson	9	J. Dempsey	5	(2)
P. Osgood	9	C. Garland	5	
D. Webb	9	P. Mulligan	5	
P. Bonetti	8	M. Hinton	4	
C. Cooke	7	E. McCreadie	1	(1)
P. Houseman	7	J. Phillips	1	

Goalscorers: Baldwin 4, Hollins 4, Osgood 4, Garland 2, Hudson 2, Cooke 1, Houseman 1, Webb 1. **Total** 19.

[EUROPEAN CUP-WINNERS' CUP]

(1)	Jeunesse (Lexembourg)	(A) W	8–0
(1)	Jeunesse	(H) W	13–0
	(Won 21–0 on aggregate)		
(2)	Atvidaberg (Sweden)	(A) D	0–0
(2)	Atvidaberg	(H) D	1–1
	(Lost on away goal)		

P. Bonetti	4	D. Webb	4	
J. Boyle	4	T. Baldwin	3	
C. Cooke	4	P. Houseman	3	
R. Harris	4	M. Hinton	2	(2)
J. Hollins	4	J. Dempsey	2	
A. Hudson	4	P. Mulligan	1	(1)
P. Osgood	4	E. McCreadie	1	

Goalscorers: Osgood 8, Baldwin 4, Houseman 3, Hollins 2, Hudson 2, Webb 2, Harris 1. **Total** 22.

SEASON 1972–73

[F.A. CUP]

(3)	Brighton & H. A.	(A)	W	2–0
(4)	Ipswich T.	(H)	W	2–0
(5)	Sheffield W.	(A)	W	2–1
(6)	Arsenal	(H)	D	2–2
(R)	Arsenal	(A)	L	1–2

J. Hollins	5	M. Hinton	3	(1)
A. Hudson	5	C. Garland	3	
S. Kember	5	R. Harris	3	
P. Osgood	5	G. Locke	3	
J. Phillips	5	E. McCreadie	3	
J. Dempsey	4	D. Webb	2	
W. Garner	4	T. Baldwin	1	
P. Houseman	4			

Goalscorers: Osgood 4, Garner 3, Hollins 1, Houseman 1. **Total** 9.

[FOOTBALL LEAGUE CUP]

(2)	Southend U.	(A)	W	1–0	(S-f 1)	Norwich C.	(H)	L	0–2
(3)	Derby Co.	(A)	D	0–0	(S-f 2)	Norwich C.	(A)		2–3
(R)	Derby Co	(H)	W	3–2		(Abandoned 84 minutes—fog)			
(4)	Bury	(A)	W	1–0	(S-f 2)	Norwich C.	(A)	L	0–1
(5)	Notts Co.	(H)	W	3–1		(Lost 0–3 on aggregate)			

R. Harris	7	A. Hudson	3
J. Hollins	7	T. Baldwin	2
P. Osgood	7	J. Boyle	2
D. Webb	7	J. Phillips	2
C. Garland	6	M. Hinton	1(1)
P. Houseman	6	J. Dempsey	1
S. Kember	6	M. Droy	1
G. Locke	6	I. Hutchinson	1
E. McCreadie	6	P. Mulligan	1
P. Bonetti	5		

Goalscorers: Garland 3, Kember 2, Osgood 2, Webb 1. **Total** 8.

CHELSEA 1973-74: RESULTS, SCORERS, CROWDS IN LEAGUE, LEAGUE CUP & F.A. CUP

1	Sat. Aug. 25	Derby	Away	L0-1		30,666
2	Tues. Aug. 28	Burnley	Away	L0-1		23,818
3	Sat. Sept. 1	Sheff. United	Home	L1-2	Hollins (pen)	27,972
4	Wed. Sept. 5	Birmingham	Home	W3-1	Hutchinson, Hollins, Kember.	25,660
5	Sat. Sept. 8	Liverpool	Away	L0-1		47,016
6	Tues. Sept. 11	Birmingham	Away	W4-2	Hudson, Osgood, Baldwin 2	30,252
7	Sat. Sept. 15	Coventry	Home	W1-0	Osgood	30,593
8	Sat. Sept. 22	Man. City	Away	L2-3	Baldwin 2	32,118
9	Sat. Sept. 29	Wolves	Home	D2-2	Garner, Osgood	27,846
10	Sat. Oct. 6	Q.P.R.	Away	D1-1	Mancini own goal	31,009
11	Mon. Oct. 8	(2LC) Stoke	Away	L0-1		17,281
12	Sat. Oct. 13	Ipswich	Home	L2-3	Baldwin, Hollins	25,111
13	Sat. Oct. 20	Newcastle	Away	L0-2		32,154
14	Fri. Oct. 26	Norwich	Home	W3-0	Baldwin 2, Kember	21,953
15	Sat. Nov. 3	Man. United	Away	D2-2	Baldwin, Osgood	48,036
16	Sat. Nov. 10	Everton	Home	W3-1	Baldwin, Osgood 2	26,398
17	Sat. Nov. 17	Arsenal	Away	D0-0		38,677
18	Sat. Nov. 24	Southampton	Home	W4-0	Britton, Garland, Kember 2	22,596
19	Sat. Dec. 8	Leicester	Home	W3-2	Hollins 2 (2 pens) Osgood	20,676
20	Sat. Dec. 15	Leeds	Home	L1-2	Osgood	40,768
21	Sat. Dec. 22	Wolves	Away	L0-2		20,837
22	Wed. Dec. 26	West Ham	Home	L2-4	Britton, Hudson	26,982
23	Sat. Dec. 29	Liverpool	Home	L0-1		32,901
24	Tues. Jan 1	Sheff. United	Away	W2-1	Kember, Hollins	32,575
25	Sat. Jan. 5	(3FAC) Q.P.R.	Home	D0-0		31,540
26	Sat. Jan. 12	Coventry	Away	D2-2	Harris, Garland	20,813
27	Tues. Jan. 15	(3FAC) Q.P.R.	Away	L0-1		28,573
28	Sat. Jan. 19	Derby	Home	D1-1	Garner	27,185
29	Sun. Jan. 27	Stoke	Away	L0-1		31,985
30	Sat. Feb. 2	Leeds	Away	D1-1	Garner	41,510
31	Sat. Feb. 9	Man. City	Home	W1-0	Webb	20,206
32	Sat. Feb. 23	Q.P.R.	Home	D3-3	Cooke, Garner 2	34,264
33	Tues. Feb. 26	Ipswich	Away	D1-1	Garland	22,415
34	Sat. Mar. 2	West Ham	Away	L0-3		34,043
35	Sat. Mar. 9	Norwich	Away	D2-2	Houseman, Kember	19,866
36	Wed. Mar. 13	Burnley	Home	W3-0	Kember, Houseman, Hutchinson	8,171
37	Sat. Mar. 16	Newcastle	Home	W1-0	Hutchinson	24,207
38	Sat. Mar. 23	Everton	Away	D1-1	Garner	29,542
39	Sat. Mar. 30	Man. United	Home	L1-3	Garner	29,602
40	Wed. Apr. 3	Tottenham	Away	W2-1	Droy, Harris	23,646
41	Sat. Apr. 6	Southampton	Away	D 0-0		27,268
42	Sat. Apr. 13	Arsenal	Home	L 1-3	Swain	29,152
43	Mon. Apr. 15	Tottenham	Home	D 0-0		26,258
44	Sat. Apr. 20	Leicester	Away	L 0-3		22,828
45	Sat. Apr. 27	Stoke	Home	L 0-1		17,150